SALTED CARAMEL DREAMS

SALTED CARAMEL DREAMS

Over 70 Incredible Caramel Creations

Chloe Timms

hardie grant books

CONTENTS

The Story of Fatties

I should have seen Fatties in my stars.

As a child, I was obsessed with sweets – whether eating them from soggy paper bags or stealing change to buy pick 'n' mix from the village shop. None of this has changed as I have grown up: reading recipe books from back to front, starting with the puddings and bakes, folding down pages and scribbling in margins; mains and starters decided upon only after dessert is determined; the sweet drawer in the kitchen fully loaded and the obligatory packet of biscuits hidden in my bedside cabinet. Through life's ups and downs, sugar has been my constant, and it has taken me all the way to my very own Fatties Bakery.

Being a self-taught baker means that I have learnt to cook with flavours that I enjoy. I believe that it is impossible to cook something really delicious unless you can't wait to eat it or share it. Conducting the magical transformation from white sugar to dark, smoking caramel and taking it on so many journeys is a joy that I will never tire of, and is something I hope you will come to love too.

I wanted to make a book that demystifies caramel – that turns it from something mystical and scary to something you'll be whipping up with confidence and imagination. Caramel is such a versatile confection – once you've mastered the basics, you can go on and experiment to your heart's content.

To begin, I'll guide you through the basic equipment, ingredients and techniques needed to make caramel successfully; how to store caramel; and what to do when things go wrong. Once you have mastered the basics, you can tread your own path into sticky greatness.

In the Cornerstones chapter (see pages 27–55), you'll find all the basic recipes and techniques that you'll need to move forward through the book. Many of the recipes throughout the book refer back to these essentials. But that's not to say the recipes are totally inflexible. Caramel sauces (see pages 32–33) can be used interchangeably in most cases or flavoured however you like. The same goes with the use of sea salt. I use a large crystal, Welsh, white sea salt and I have given my recommended amounts, but if you love things really salty, add another pinch, or pull back a little if it's not your thing. There's a fantastic range of salts available in speciality stores; have a play to find your perfect partner.

Once you have all this under your belt, you can move on to Fatties greatness! Build a fort of Cornflake Bocaditos (see page 58), thrill friends and family alike with gooey Goldmine Brownies (see page 84), or throw a full-on Fatties party, complete with cocktails and cake!

Whatever you do, go forth with an appetite and indulge in your salted caramel dreams…

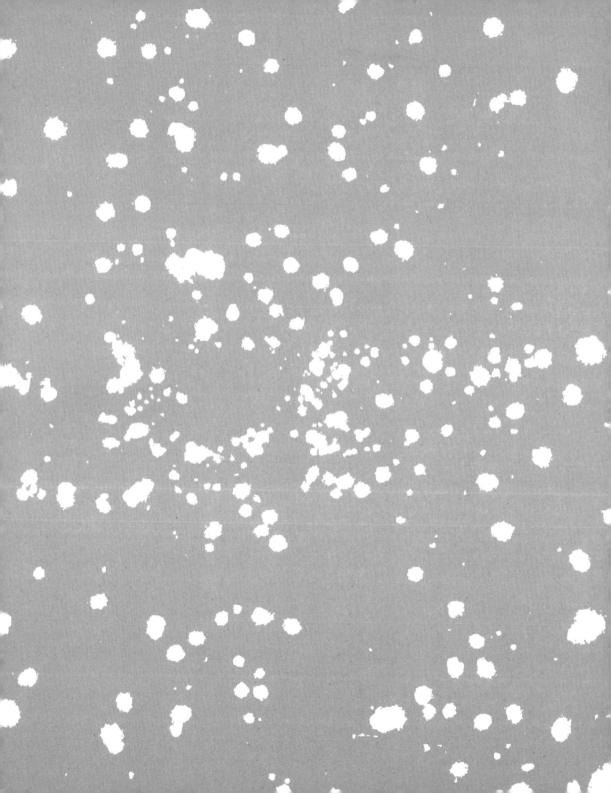

Techniques + Equipment

Just a few pages of me being bossy,
then we can get on to the fun stuff!

Ingredients

Store cupboard essentials to start you on your sticky journey.

SEA SALTS

There are many different varieties of sea salt – experiment to find your favourite flavour profile. When fine sea salt is required use a fine ground sea salt or grind your own in a pestle and mortar. NEVER USE TABLE SALT.

DAIRY

Always use the best dairy products you can. The tastier the cream and butter you start with, the tastier the finished product.

SUGARS

Caster (superfine) sugar forms the base of most caramels. It has a small grain that easily liquefies. Darker sugars can add caramel flavour to a recipe without the actual inclusion of caramel.

INVERT SUGARS

Invert sugars are mixtures of glucose and fructose. I like to use glucose syrup in my caramels for a clean flavour, but you can also use other inverts such as golden (light corn) syrup and treacle. Temperatures may need to be adjusted if substituting glucose syrup for natural inverts such as honey and maple syrup in recipes such as Classic Chewy Salted Caramels (see page 28).

VANILLA

Vanilla pods, seeds and extracts are perfect for flavouring, but never use essence – it can taste bitter and synthetic.

CHOCOLATE

Use the best chocolate you can. Dark should have at least 70 per cent cocoa solids, milk between 38 and 40 per cent, and white should have a minimum 30 per cent cocoa solids. Never use anything marked as 'chocolate coating' or 'chocolate-flavoured'.

Equipment

~

There are just a few items that you need before you get started on your caramel adventure.

HEATPROOF SILICONE SPATULAS

Heatproof spatulas are imperative when cooking at high temperatures to avoid molten plastic. Caramel can easily stick to wooden spoons but chips right off silicone.

HIGH TEMPERATURE DIGITAL THERMOMETER

A digital, instant-read probe or thermometer makes reading temperatures easy and clear. Unlike old-fashioned sugar thermometers, there isn't a submersion level, making it easy to measure small quantities as well as large.

LARGE, HEAVY-BASED PAN

This should have at least a 7-litre (12-pint) capacity. Heavy-based pans are great for even heat distribution. A light-coloured pan is perfect for making caramel as you can easily observe the colour changes; however, you just can't beat a copper sugar pan for perfect caramel cookery.

MINI BLOWTORCH

Strictly non-essential but super fun for toasting and charring all things mallow.

HEATPROOF PASTRY BRUSH

Great for washing away errant sugar crystals.

PORTIONERS

A set of metallic sprung-handled portioners is a great way to equally divide cookie doughs and batters to achieve uniform results.

SET OF MEASURING SPOONS AND A MINI MEASURING JUG

Useful for measuring small amounts of wet and dry ingredients.

SHARP, LONG-BLADED KNIFE

Makes slicing up chewy caramels a snip.

STAINLESS STEEL RULER

Extremely useful for neatly cutting caramels and their wrappings. Stainless steel rulers are durable and hygienic.

WHISK

A good whisk is essential for achieving smooth batters, sauces and custards.

Mise en Place

I have my neurotic moments, but trust me this isn't one of them. Being organised and having everything weighed out, laid out and to hand will make you the best caramel cook.

Things can move quickly when working with caramel. The last thing you want to be doing is running to the other side of the kitchen, grabbing the cream, weighing it out, warming it and only then being ready to add it to the cooking sugar.

Not only is it dangerous to leave a pan of hot sugar unattended, it's possible that your caramel could turn from perfection to burnt in a matter of seconds, forcing you to start over.

You should always work calmly around caramel; you don't want to be sploshing things about in a panicked hurry.

The same should apply to equipment: it is useful to have clean set of spatulas, pans and cloths to hand.

Most importantly, this way of cooking leaves you calm, organised and ready to enjoy the joys, excitement and transformations of caramel making.

Techniques + Equipment ~ p.15

Dry Caramel

〜

My first attempt to make a dry caramel was aged ten, standing at the stove stirring a dry pot of salt for two hours, mystified as to why nothing was happening. I'm still embarrassed it took me so long to realise it was salt.

As I taught myself to bake, caramel was the one thing I was terrified to conquer. All the books I read barked warnings of crystallised sugar and burnt hands, disasters unknown and pans awaiting ruin. Eventually I summoned up all my courage and gave it a go, following instructions to make a wet caramel, reportedly a good place to start. It crystallised, but I cracked on and researched why this was happening. I went to a DIY store and bought a paintbrush and brushed down the sides of the pan to wash away sugar crystals as they formed, practising until I perfected the technique (for the perfect Wet Caramel, see page 18). My apprenticeship over, I moved on to dry caramel. It was perfect the first

time. I could bash the sugar around and stir to my heart's content. Caramel wasn't a big bad fiddly beast, it was a dream. Dry caramel remains my favourite method to make a quick, dark caramel suitable for most recipes in this book.

Here's the science: sugar, when independently heated above 160°C (320°F), undergoes an irreversible state change known as caramelisation. The water content of sucrose sugars (most common white sugars) allows the sugar to liquify easily, meaning that it's easy to caramelise sugar without the addition of any extra liquid and the sugar is less likely to crystallise. In short, that means it's OK TO STIR!

Method

Add the sugar to a heavy-based saucepan and shake out to an even layer.

Heat over a medium heat for 1–2 minutes until patches of sugar begin to liquify. Stir to coat the dry sugar in the liquified sugar. The sugar will clump, but don't panic! Keep stirring, mixing and breaking up the clumps of sugar as it liquefies and caramelises. The sugar will be fully liquid and starting to turn dark after 5–6 minutes. For a light to medium caramel, pull the pan off the heat just before all the lumps have melted, while stirring to allow the heat of the pan to melt the remaining sugar. For a dark caramel, continue to cook, stirring, until smooth, smoking and just starting to foam – depending on the colour desired, this will take another 1–2 minutes.

If the liquified, caramelised sugar is darkening too fast, before all the lumps are melted, simply reduce the heat slightly and continue as before.

The more sugar you have to caramelise, the longer this technique will take and the more you will have to stir and bash – but that's half the fun!

Ingredients

250 g (9 oz/generous 1 cup) caster (superfine) sugar (but you can use any quantity)

Wet Caramel

~

Making a wet caramel can be a tricky and frustrating affair. If you stir it or allow any crystals to form, you'll end up throwing the pan at the wall. Been there. Although the crystallised sugar formations can be rather beautiful, they do not make a caramel.

With a few simple tricks, however, all this mess and bother can be avoided. By adding a small amount of inverted sugar (which is a mixture of glucose and fructose) to the sugar and water, you inhibit the re-growth of sugar crystals. I like to use glucose syrup as it imparts no flavour to the finished caramel, but other inverts such as golden (light corn) syrup, honey and maple syrup will work just as well. Start with a really clean pan and equipment free of any impurities.

Sugar crystals love to get together and their microscopic rough edges easily attach to each other and grow. Another easy way to avoid crystals is to have a cup of warm water and a pastry brush to hand, then simply wash away any undissolved sugar from the side of the pan.

The stages of a wet caramel are easier to observe than dry caramel and control (see previous page), making it perfect for lighter tones of caramel as well as very dark.

Method

In a large saucepan, dissolve the sugar and glucose in the water, stirring to help the sugar to dissolve. Use a wet pastry brush to wash away any grains of sugar remaining on the inside of the pan.

Over a medium-high heat, bring the sugar mixture to the boil, then boil for 5–10 minutes until light golden or smoking and dark as desired.

Use as directed in the recipes.

Ingredients

225 g (8 oz/1 cup) caster (superfine) sugar

3 tbsp glucose syrup

4 tbsp water

Sterilising + Filling

Jars of Salted Caramel Peanut Butter (see page 62) and caramel sauces (see pages 32–33) make wonderful homemade gifts. Even better when they contain no nasty bacteria! Enter sterilisation.

To sterilise your jars, preheat the oven to 140°C (275°F/Gas 1) and bring a saucepan of water to the boil. Wash the jars and lids thoroughly in hot soapy water and rinse well, ensuring no traces of soap remain. Place the jars on a baking sheet, not touching, and bake for 20 minutes. The jars should be bone dry when removed from the oven. While the jars are in the oven, boil the lids for 15 minutes before removing with a pair of clean metal tongs to air-dry upside down on a clean cooling rack.

It's important to make sure that the jar and the contents you are putting in it are at the same temperature to avoid the glass cracking or shattering. Hot in hot jars and cold in cold jars. Jar caramel sauce when it is hot, but wait for the jars to cool before filling with the salted caramel peanut butter.

A clean piping bag or two sterilised metal spoons (follow instructions as for lids) are perfect for getting the peanut butter into the jar. For the salted caramel sauces, a wide funnel is brilliant to avoid spills.

As soon as the jars are full, tightly screw on the lids straight away. Store as instructed in the recipe.

Cutting + Wrapping

~

I am often asked how I cut my Classic Chewy Salted (see page 28) so cleanly. The trick is to cut the caramels when they are only just set, so here are a few indications of when that might be.

Setting times vary due to ambient temperature, humidity and cooking temperature, which can be anywhere from 1–4 hours. Caramels cooked at a higher temperature will set faster than caramels cooked at a lower temperature. If the ambient room temperature is cold, this will speed up the setting time, and vice versa if warm. But note: any kind of caramel hates humidity! If the environment is damp, wrap the caramels as quickly as possible to avoid a sticky mess.

Cut the caramels on a clean, flat chopping board with a sharp, long-bladed knife and stainless steel ruler.

Caramels must be wrapped before being stored. In the UK it's really hard to find pre-made wrappers, so I make my own. Doing it this way also means you can whip up a batch of caramels and wrap them without the need for specialist wrappers. Depending on the size of your cut caramels, you will need 70–80 wrappers per baking sheet.

The best and most effective way to make the wrappers is to cut 5–7.5 cm (2½–3 in) squares out of parchment paper on a clean cutting mat using a scalpel and stainless steel ruler.

To wrap the caramels, take one caramel and one wrapper, then place the caramel three-quarters of the way down the paper in the middle (as shown). Fold up the shorter piece of paper to cover the caramel and continue to roll up tightly. Holding the wrapped caramel in one hand, pinch one end of the overhanging paper and twist to secure. Flip and twist the other side. Continue until all the caramels are wrapped.

Safety + Troubleshooting

Although I want to show you how simple caramel is to make, there are a few words of advice I should impart before we begin.

BE SAFE. CARAMEL IS HOT, PLEASE BE CAREFUL

Until you are a confident caramel maker, it is prudent to cover your hands (and arms, if you are super clumsy) with oven mitts, but be sure they have a good grip. Wear tight-fitting sleeves that are unlikely to catch on pan handles and send molten sugar flying.

If hot caramel splashes onto your skin, it will cool and harden very quickly. Remove the caramel from your skin as soon as possible and run the affected area under tepid water for 20–30 minutes. If the burn is very bad, seek immediate professional medical help.

When adding liquids to caramel, the mixture is likely to bubble, spit and steam. Stand well back after any additions and only stir once the bubbling has subsided. If lots of liquid is being added – as in the Simple Caramel Syrup (see page 50) – I would recommend covering your hand with a mitt to avoid the risk of a steam burn.

THE SMOKE ALARMS ARE RINGING AND MY EYES ARE BURNING!

If not monitored, caramel can easily burn. That's just a fact and in no way do I want that to put you off. But it's a fact.

There's a fine line between wonderfully dark, smoky caramel verging on burnt, and actually burnt. If, when trying to find this sweet spot, you do burn a pan of caramel, don't panic. Very calmly and carefully remove the pan from the heat, wait for a few seconds for the caramel to stop bubbling ferociously, then pour out the burnt caramel onto a sheet of baking parchment or a silicone mat on a baking sheet. Leave it to set and then dispose of it.

As for the pan, it is salvageable: simply wait for it to cool before filling with water and bringing to the boil, which will dissolve the caramel.

MY CARAMEL IS PALE AND LACKING THE FLAVOUR I WANT

The colour of caramel is a sliding scale in parallel with its flavour profile. How you like it is up to you. For the recipes in this book, I have recommended the colour of the caramel I prefer, but you can adjust this to your taste.

However, if you want to experience the wonderful bitterness of a really dark caramel but can somehow never achieve it and keep pulling off pans of pale, straw-coloured caramel, here is why: you are not being brave enough. Cook the caramel for a little longer than you feel comfortable with, remembering that what can be confused with smoke is often the evaporation of water. If you burn a couple of pans along the way, it's ok. After all, you've got to crack a few eggs to make an omelette.

MY CARAMELS WON'T SET

Exact temperature is a key player in the Classic Chewy Salted Caramels recipe (see page 28) as well as Marshmallow Fluff (see page 52) and Malted Mallows (see page 68). If things aren't quite right, it's most likely that your thermometer isn't properly calibrated.

To recalibrate your thermometer, bring a small pan of water to a boil. Insert the thermometer, making sure not to touch the sides or bottom of the pan. It should read 100°C (212°F) (at sea level). If it registers a few degrees out, you can add or subtract this difference from the desired temperature.

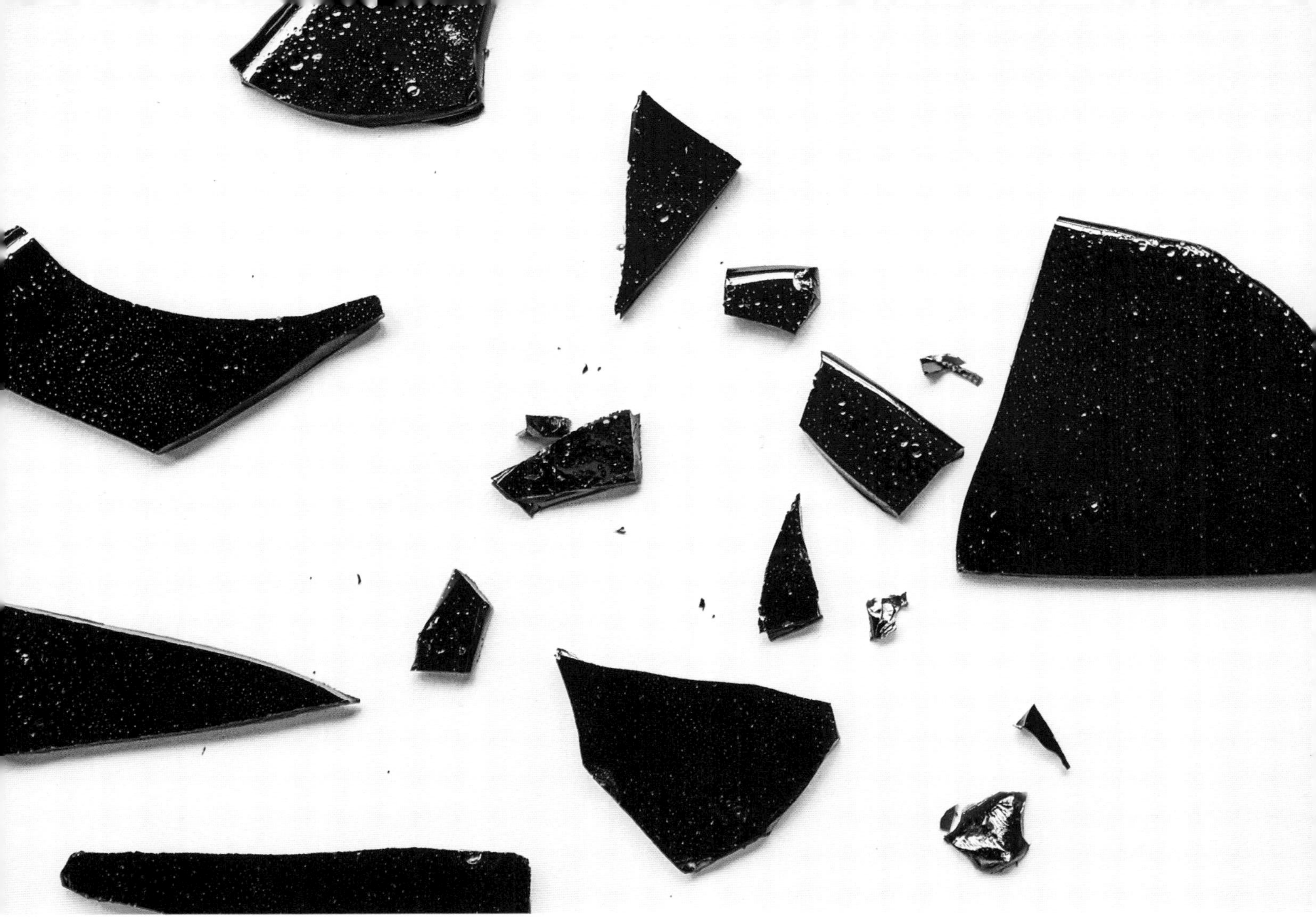

Cornerstones

Get these recipes down to level up.

Classic Chewy Salted Caramels

~

I first made these caramels for a Christmas market in east London. Some almost cracked teeth and others leaked from the wrappings. But however they came, people went nuts for them! I've since improved my techniques and these remain a Fatties headliner. I have given two different setting temperatures in the recipe: a lower one for a softer caramel and a higher one for a chewier caramel.

Makes a 20 cm (8 in) square pan to cut into 70 caramels

Cornerstones ~ p.28

Lightly butter a 20 cm (8 in) square baking sheet, line with baking parchment and lightly grease the paper too. You can also use similar-sized silicone cake moulds.

In a small saucepan, gently melt together the cream, glucose, salt and half the sugar. Bring almost to the boil but do not allow the mixture to boil. Remove from the heat, cover and keep warm.

In a large, heavy-based saucepan, make a dark dry caramel with the remaining sugar (see page 16). Once smoking, add the butter and stir to incorporate, watching out for bubbles and splutters. Turn the heat down to medium-low and slowly pour in the warmed cream mixture, stirring to combine. Continue to cook until the temperature reaches 122–124°C (251–255°F), ensuring the thermometer does not touch the bottom of the pan. Stir the caramel frequently to avoid hot spots and make sure it cooks evenly.

As soon as the caramel reaches the required temperature, immediately remove the pan from the heat. Stir until the bubbling subsides and the caramel is smooth. Slowly pour into the prepared pan. Leave to set before cutting and wrapping (see pages 22–23). Caramels can be stored wrapped and in an airtight container for up to 1 month.

80 g (3 oz/scant ⅓ cup) cold salted butter, cubed, plus extra for greasing

200 ml (7 fl oz/scant 1 cup) double (heavy) cream

80 g (3 oz/scant ¼ cup) glucose syrup

1½ tsp sea salt

300 g (10½ oz/1⅓ cups) caster (superfine) sugar, divided in half

CHOCOLATE SALTED CARAMELS

For chocolate caramels, increase the sea salt to 2 teaspoons. Bring the caramel to temperature, adjusting the setting temperatures to 120°C (248°F) for soft caramels and 122°C (251°F) for chewy. Remove from the heat and add 50 g (2 oz/¼ cup) finely chopped, good-quality dark chocolate, with 70% cocoa solids. Stir to combine, before pouring out into the prepared pan.

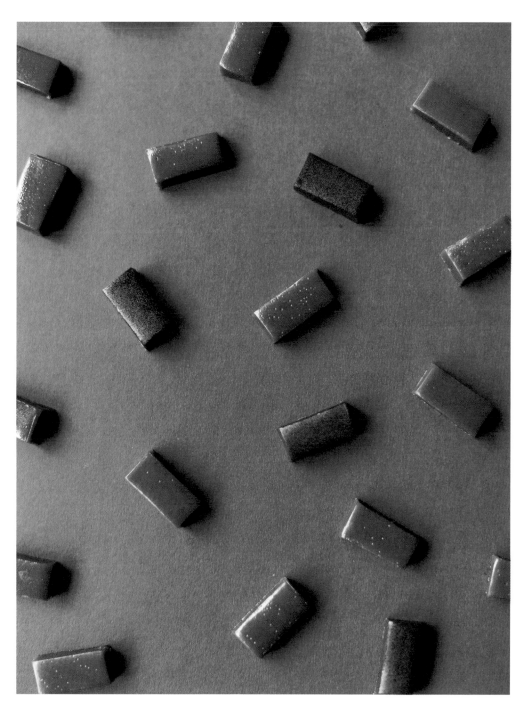

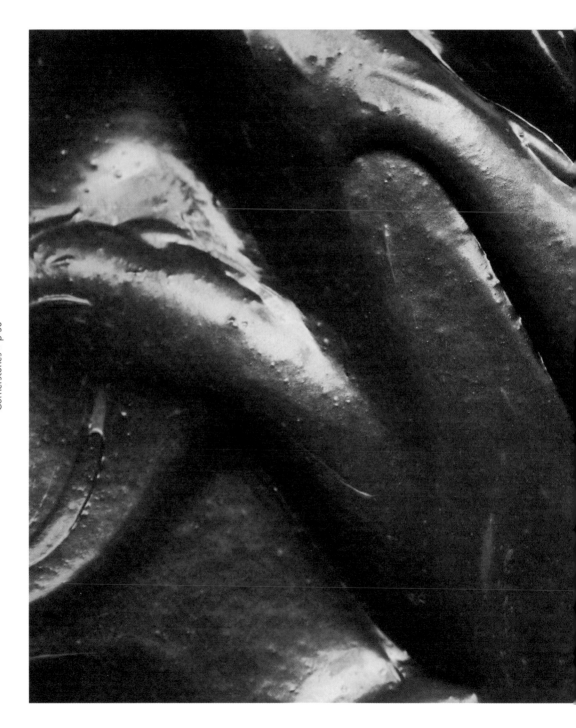

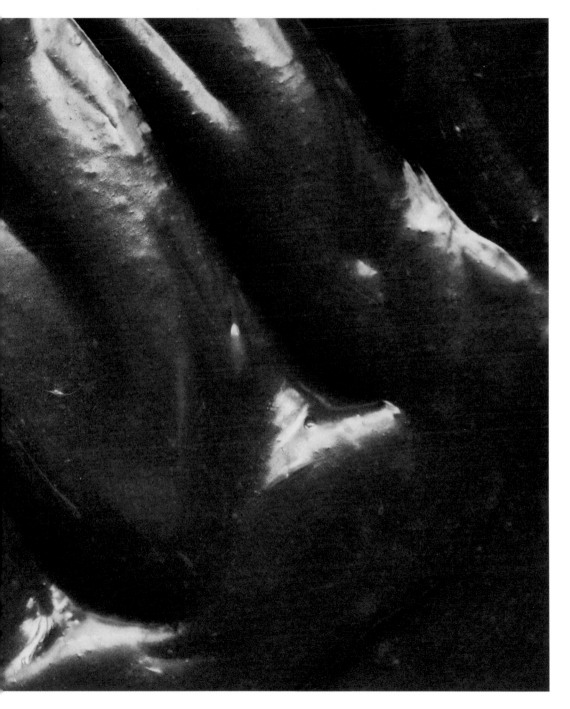

Classic Salted Caramel Sauce

Most recipes in this book rely on this mother recipe, so add it to your repertoire before you venture any further. It's such a wonderful sauce, coppery, thick and scoopable at room temperature, and silky smooth when warmed. I've noted down a few simple adaptations, but do experiment—the world is your... um ... sticky, caramel oyster.

Makes 500 g (1 lb 2 oz)

In a small saucepan, warm the cream and salt over a low heat until hot but not boiling, stirring often to avoid scorching. Alternatively, warm in the microwave in a suitable jug. Cover to keep warm while you make the caramel.

Following the instructions on pages 18–19, make a dark wet caramel with the sugar, glucose syrup and water.

Once the caramel is ready, remove from the heat and, being very careful, gradually add the warmed cream and salt. It will bubble and spit ferociously. Do not stir until the bubbles have died down.

Add the butter and stir well. If you have lumps of caramel, return to a low heat and stir until the lumps have dissolved. If not using immedietely, pour the sauce, or any of the variations below, into sterilised jars while still hot (see page 20). The sauce will keep in the fridge for up to 2 months.

200 ml (7 fl oz/scant 1 cup) double (heavy) cream

¾ tsp sea salt

225 g (8 oz/1 cup) caster (superfine) sugar

3 tbsp glucose syrup

4 tbsp water

65 g (2½ oz/generous ¼ cup) salted butter

CHOCOLATE SALTED CARAMEL SAUCE

For a thick chocolate caramel sauce, add 65 g (2¼ oz/scant ½ cup) good-quality dark chocolate to the caramel after the butter has been added.

MISO SALTED CARAMEL SAUCE

For a salty miso caramel sauce, leave out the sea salt and add 1–2 tablespoons sweet white miso paste after the butter has been added.

BROWN BUTTER SALTED CARAMEL SAUCE

Following the instructions on page 54, make a brown butter using the quantity of butter specified in the recipe plus 2 teaspoons. Leave to cool in the pan, then, once solidified, scrape out, wrap in parchment and refrigerate until ready to use. Use as directed in the recipe to replace the salted butter.

MALTY CARAMEL SAUCE

For a rich, malty caramel sauce add 1–2 tablespoons malt syrup after the butter has been added. Alternatively, boil a bottle of your favourite ale in a large pan until syrupy, then add 1–2 tablespoons of the ale syrup instead.

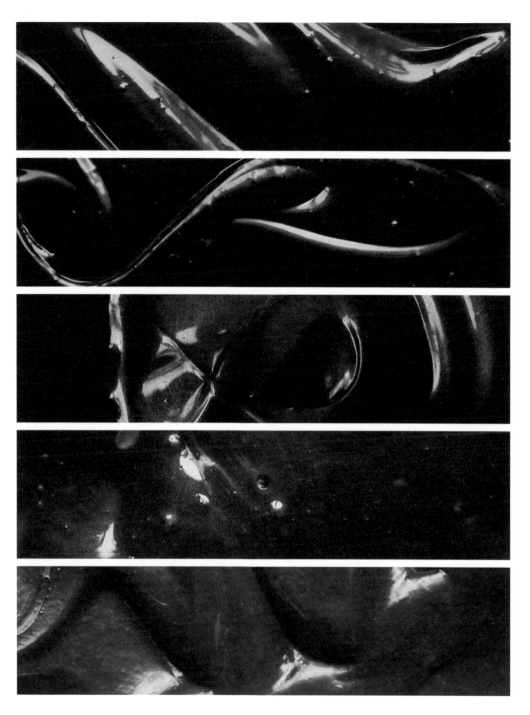

Dulce de Leche

~

Dulce de leche is a caramel confection made by slowly cooking sweetened cow's milk. As with Brown Butter (see page 54), it relies on the Maillard reaction. To assist with that reaction, I like to add bicarbonate of soda at the start of the cooking process to increase the pH and aid the browning process to create a really complex flavour. I could go into the reasons behind this, but do you really want me to ramble on about amino acids? Thought not! I use dulce de leche to fill my Alfajores (see page 100) but it's wonderful spread or drizzled over almost anything that needs an extra special sweet touch.

Makes 500 g (1 lb 2 oz)

In a 7-litre (12-pint) saucepan, combine the milk, sugar and bicarbonate of soda and whisk together to dissolve the sugar.

Set the pan over a medium heat and bring to a shimmering simmer. Keep a very close eye on the pan at this stage as the liquid will foam up considerably.

Turn down the heat and keep at a low simmer for 45 minutes–1 hour, whisking occasionally to begin with and more often towards the end as it starts to thicken, to stop it from catching.

Once thickened and dark, remove from the heat and add the sea salt, then leave to cool before using. Alternatively, pour into sterilised jars while still hot (see page 20). The sauce will keep in the fridge for up to 1 month.

1 litre (34 fl oz/4⅓ cups) full-fat (whole) milk

200 g (7oz/scant 1 cup) caster (superfine) sugar

¼ tsp bicarbonate of soda (baking soda)

½ tsp sea salt

Cajeta

Cajeta, like dulce de leche, is made by reducing sweetened milk, in this case goat's milk, with added cinnamon and vanilla for spice. It's awesome spread over fresh crusty bread or as a dip for juicy strawberries. If you can get hold of some cones of piloncillo sugar, you are in for a real treat. (It is available to buy online, but you don't even want to know the price!) An unrefined Mexican sugar made from boiling cane juice, its smoky, earthy tones really enrich this recipe, adding further notes of deep caramel. For a very smooth cajeta, opt for UHT milk or ultra pasteurised goat's milk, which is available at most supermarkets. Goat's milk doesn't contain as much lactose as cow's milk so isn't as likely to catch, meaning you don't have to watch it like a hawk until you are nearing the end of the cooking process, unlike dulce de leche. See photo on page 34.

Makes about 400 g (14 oz)

In a large saucepan, stir together the piloncillo, goat's milk and bicarbonate of soda until the sugar has dissolved. Add the cinnamon stick. Scrape the vanilla seeds into the pan, then add the scraped pod.

Very slowly bring the mixture to a gentle simmer. It will foam up considerably so keep a close eye on it. At no point do you want the milk to boil, but keep it at a bare simmer for 1–1½ hours. Keep a good eye on the pan and stir every so often. After this time, the mixture will be thickened and turning a light golden brown.

Now it's time to pay close attention. The cajeta will cook and catch quickly at this stage so it is best to stir constantly as this also allows you to gauge the desired consistency. For a pourable sauce, stop cooking when the mixture just coats the back of a spoon. For a spreadable texture, cook for slightly longer until a thicker coating is left, but always bear in mind the cajeta will thicken considerably when cooled.

Remove from the heat and add the sea salt, then leave to cool before using or store in sterilised jars (see page 20).

250 g (9 oz/generous 1 cup) piloncillo, grated (or good-quality dark soft brown sugar)

1 litre (34 fl oz/4⅓ cups) full-fat (whole) goat's milk

¼ tsp bicarbonate of soda (baking soda)

1 cinnamon stick

1 small or ½ large vanilla pod (bean), split

½ tsp sea salt

Goat's Curd Butterscotch Sauce

Don't be put off by the use of goat's curd in this recipe. It adds a much-needed tangy earthiness that rounds out the richness. Perfect served with Brown Butterscotch Cups (see page 115).

Makes about 400 g (14 oz)

In a small saucepan, melt together the butter, sugar, cream and goat's curd over a low heat.

Once melted, turn the heat up slightly and bring to a very gentle boil for 4–5 minutes, whisking all the time. The butterscotch should darken and thicken.

Whisk in the vanilla extract, then allow to cool slightly before tasting for seasoning. Depending on the saltiness of the curds, you may or may not need extra salt.

Store in an airtight container in the fridge for up to 2 weeks. Heat in a pan over a low heat to bring back to a pouring consistency.

110 g (3¾ oz/scant ½ cup) salted butter

110 g (3¾ oz/½ cup) dark soft brown sugar

100 ml (3½ fl oz/scant ½ cup) double (heavy) cream

110 g (3¾ oz/scant ½ cup) fresh goat's curd

1 tsp vanilla extract

a pinch of sea salt, to taste

Tahini Caramel

This thick caramel holds enough body to be stuffed between cookies (see Tahini Cookies, page 97). Its slightly bitter, nutty flavour makes it a natural partner to anything chocolate.

Makes 450 g (1 lb)

In a small saucepan, warm the cream and salt until hot but not boiling, stirring often to avoid scorching. Cover to keep warm.

In a large, heavy-based saucepan, make a dark dry caramel with the sugar (see page 16). Once dark and smoking, remove it from the heat and add the butter; it will splutter. Stir once the spluttering has subsided. Add the tahini and stir well. Finish by adding the warmed cream and salt, mixing well.

Store in an airtight container in the fridge for up to 2 months. Heat in a pan over a low heat to bring back to a pouring consistency.

150 ml (5 fl oz/scant ⅔ cup) double (heavy) cream

½ tsp sea salt

225 g (8 oz/1 cup) caster (superfine) sugar

30 g (1 oz/2 tbsp) salted butter

70 g (2¼ oz/generous ¼ cup) tahini paste

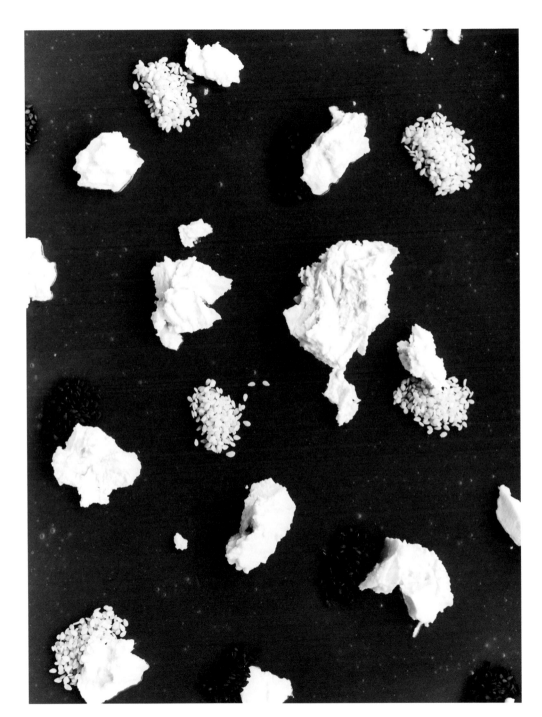

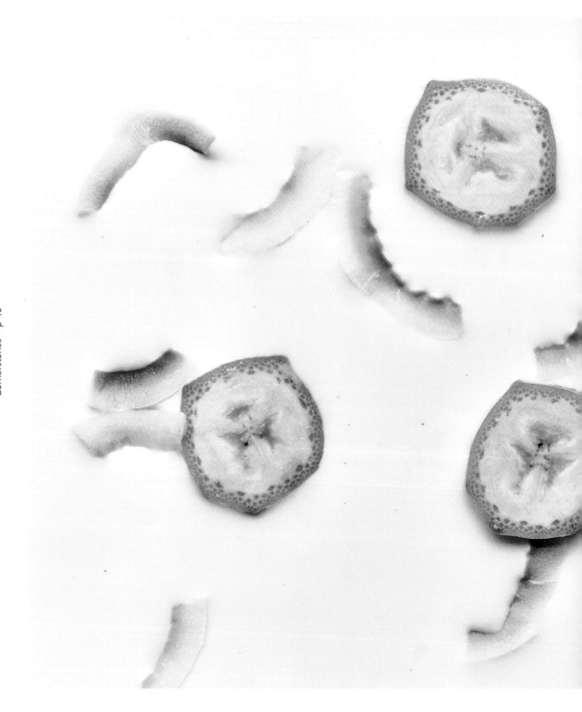

Vegan Coconut Caramel Sauce

When it came to making a vegan caramel sauce I wanted to avoid all fakery. Enter three coconut products with different properties: creamed coconut, high in fat, acting as a butter substitute; coconut milk for body; and coconut cream for rich silkiness.

Makes 600 g (1 lb 5 oz)

In a medium, heavy-based saucepan, make a dark dry caramel with the sugar (see page 16). Once the caramel is smoking and beginning to foam, remove the pan from the heat, tip in the creamed coconut and stir until almost fully melted. Carefully add the coconut milk and coconut cream, watching out for steam and spluttering.

Return to the heat and slowly bring to the boil, mixing well so that all the ingredients are well incorporated and the sauce is smooth. Add the sea salt and boil for 5 minutes or until slightly thickened.

Serve warm or leave to cool completely before refrigerating. The sauce can be stored for 1 month in an airtight container in the fridge. When chilled, the caramel will become opaque, but once warmed will return to a shiny golden brown. Heat in a pan over a low heat to bring back to a pouring consistency.

200 g (7 oz/scant 1 cup) caster (superfine) sugar

50 g (2 oz/scant ¼ cup) sachet creamed coconut, roughly chopped

400 ml (124 fl oz) tinned full-fat coconut milk

160 ml (5¼ fl oz/⅔ cup) tinned coconut cream

1 tsp sea salt

Bananas Foster Caramel Sauce

This was a recipe that came together fortuitously with a cup of this and a dash of that – it needed no tweaking. It was love at first lick. I used it as a topping for brownies and cream at my stall at Meatopia – an annual festival of meat held in London – along with the Crunchy Maple Bacon Popcorn (see page 66) and it was such a success I had to include it in this book. I add the rum off the heat to retain the alcohol but feel free to burn it off or leave it out for a kid-friendly sauce.

Makes 450 g (1 lb)

In a small saucepan, warm the cream, salt and cinnamon until hot but not boiling, stirring often to avoid scorching. Whisk well to combine, but don't worry if the cinnamon is clumpy. Alternatively, warm the mixture in the microwave in a suitable jug. Cover to keep warm while you make the caramel.

In a large, heavy-based saucepan, make a medium-dark dry caramel with the sugar (see page 16). Reduce the heat to low and add the chopped banana, stirring to coat in the caramel. Gradually add the warmed cream mixture, stirring only once the bubbles have subsided. Remove from the heat and leave to cool for 5 minutes.

Add the vanilla extract and rum and stir well, then blend until smooth, using a handheld or standard blender.

Use warm or leave to cool completely before refrigerating. The sauce can be stored for 2 weeks in an airtight container in the fridge. Heat in a pan over a low heat to bring back to a pouring consistency.

250 ml (8½ fl oz/1 cup) double (heavy) cream

1 tsp sea salt

½ tsp ground cinnamon

225 g (8 oz/1 cup) caster (superfine) sugar

1 large ripe banana, chopped

½ tsp vanilla extract

2–4 tbsp dark rum

Caramel Sugar

~

This sugar is a great way to add caramel flavour to a recipe without adding extra moisture, as in the Golden Macaroons (see page 70). Adding caster (superfine) sugar to the ground caramel helps to prolong the shelf life, meaning you can always have some to hand. As a general rule, use a ratio of 2:1 caramelised sugar and caster sugar to create any amount of caramel sugar.

Makes about 350 g (12 oz)

Lay a 30 × 40 cm (12 × 16 in) non-stick shallow baking sheet or silicone sheet on a large, flat, heatproof surface.

In a large, heavy-based saucepan, make a medium-dark dry caramel with two-thirds of the sugar (see page 16). Take the caramel off the heat before it becomes too dark and swirl the pan to cool the caramel slightly as the caramel continues to darken. Once just smoking, carefully pour out the caramel onto the prepared surface, scraping the sides down with a heatproof spatula to get as much out as possible.

Leave to cool and harden for about 15–20 minutes, depending on the ambient temperature.

Once set, smash up with a small toffee hammer or other small instrument of destruction. Break up into small shards and put in the bowl of a food processor fitted with the blade attachment. Add the remaining sugar and pulse with the caramel shards to a fine consistency.

Use immediately or store in an airtight container well away from moisture for up to 6 months. Heat in a pan over a low heat to bring back to a pouring consistency.

300 g (10½ oz/1⅓ cups) caster (superfine) sugar, divided into two-thirds and one-third

Caramelised White Chocolate

~

I call this 'caramelised' but strictly this is the Maillard reaction coming into play (for more on this magical reaction, see page 54). Once you make this you will never look at a sickly bar of white chocolate in the same way. But you do need the correct bar of white chocolate, with a butter fat proportion of 30 per cent or higher. As with all chocolate, the caramelised white chocolate will be solid at room temperature but warmed up will become lusciously smooth again. Follow the recipe below for an ambrosial caramelised white chocolate sauce.

Makes 300 g (10½ oz)

Preheat the oven to 120°C (250°F/Gas ½).

Spread the chocolate over a large, clean, rimmed baking sheet.

Heat for 45 minutes to 1¼ hours, stirring every 10 minutes or so until the chocolate is liquid and deeply golden, although how 'caramelised' or dark you like the chocolate is up to you.

Once coloured to your liking, season with the sea salt, if using, and pour into a clean jar or airtight container. Store at room temperature for up to 2 months. Heat in a pan over a low heat to bring back to a pouring consistency.

300 g (10½ oz/2 cups) good-quality white chocolate fêves, drops or a bar chopped into pieces

½ tsp smoked or natural sea salt (optional)

Caramelised White Chocolate Sauce

~

For a delicious hot chocolate drink, top up with 250 ml (8½ fl oz/1 cup) full-fat (whole) milk and serve in little cups.

Makes 300 g (10½ oz)

In a small saucepan over a low heat, gently heat the chocolate with the cream, stirring frequently. After about 5 minutes, the chocolate will fully melt into the cream and form a smooth sauce.

Continue to warm until hot but not boiling. Serve warm as you would a custard.

150 g (5 oz) Caramelised White Chocolate (see recipe above)

300 ml (10 fl oz/1¼ cups) double (heavy) cream

Salted Caramel Custard

~

At boarding school, we ate many a cold thing out of a tin, the best being Bird's custard, the worst being Heinz tomato soup. It's not that we weren't fed – in fact, we were fed very well. It's just that for some reason we'd find ourselves making marshmallow toasties (melts) and microwaving baked apples in honey and butter. Tinned goods could be kept easily for ages under the bed, making them perfect tucker. Looking back it was like a micro prison system, tuck being bartered like cigarettes, friendships made and broken on exchanges. Getting back on course, this custard is far from the tinned stuff and about half as sweet, with a good spike of sea salt. I think it is perfect cold from the fridge, but that might be the institutionalised child in me.

Makes about 450 ml (15 fl oz/scant 2 cups), depending on thickness

In a medium bowl, whisk together the egg yolks and one-third of the sugar to form a paste. Set to one side.

In a small saucepan, over a low heat, gently warm the cream and milk. Set to one side and cover to keep warm.

In a large, heavy-based saucepan, make a dark dry caramel with the remaining sugar (see page 16).

Whisk the butter and sea salt into the caramel, then whisk in the warm milk and cream. Remove from the heat.

Pour out about 100 ml (3½ fl oz/scant ½ cup) of the hot liquid onto the egg yolks and sugar, whisking, to thin the paste. Gradually pour this mixture back into the hot cream and milk liquid, whisking all the time.

Whisk in the vanilla seeds and return the pan to a low heat. Heat, whisking often, until the custard is thickened to a consistency you enjoy, bearing in mind that the custard will thicken more as it cools, if you like your custard chilled.

If not using straight away, remove the custard to a jug or bowl and cover with cling film (plastic wrap), pressing the film onto the surface of the custard to avoid a skin forming. Leave to cool to room temperature and then refrigerate until needed.

The custard will keep for about 3 days in an airtight container in the fridge.

6 large free-range egg yolks

150 g (5 oz/⅔ cup) caster (superfine) sugar, divided into one-third and two-thirds

250 ml (8½ fl oz/1 cup) double (heavy) cream

250 ml (8½ fl oz/1 cup) full-fat (whole) milk

30 g (1 oz/2 tbsp) unsalted butter

1 tsp sea salt

seeds from 1 vanilla pod (bean)

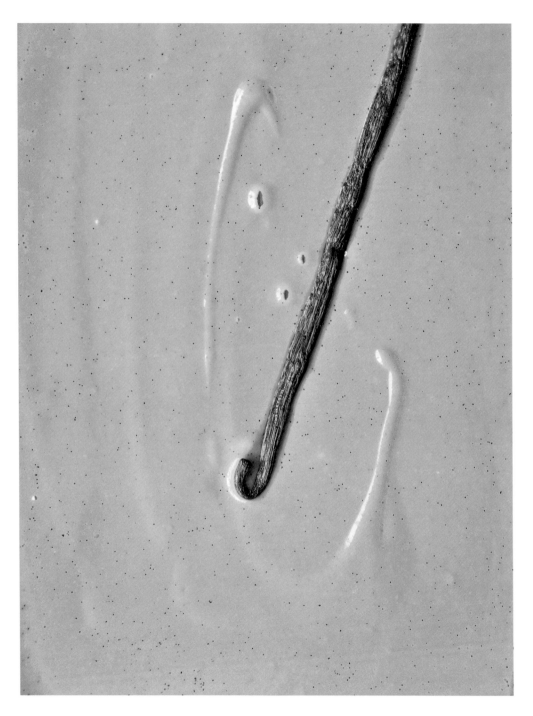

Simple Caramel Syrup

This is such a simple recipe, but is great for adding caramel flavour and sweetness to iced coffees, hot cocoa and cocktails such as the Flapjack Punch (see page 130). A warning before you begin. I like to use a dry caramel base for the syrup for the cleanest flavour, which means that when you add the water it is going to violently spit and bubble. It might be prudent to protect yourself with oven mitts to avoid a steam burn. For a sweet twist, add a vanilla pod to the syrup or for a salted caramel syrup, add a pinch of sea salt when dissolving the caramel in the water.

Makes about 450 ml (15 fl oz/scant 2 cups), depending on thickness

In a large, heavy-based saucepan, make a dark dry caramel with the sugar (see page 16).

Remove from the heat and very carefully add 50 ml (2 fl oz/¼ cup) of the water. It will bubble and splutter violently so stand well back. Very carefully add the remaining water, not stirring until the steam has subsided and the bubbles have died away.

Return to a medium heat and stir to dissolve the caramel in the water.

Remove from the heat and leave to cool slightly before pouring into a sterilised jar (see page 20).

If you like, add the vanilla seeds and scraped vanilla pod to the jar with a pinch of salt.

Store in a sterilsed jar in the fridge for up to 2 months (see page 20).

200 g (7 oz/scant 1 cup) caster (superfine) sugar

200 ml (7 fl oz/generous ¾ cup) water

1 vanilla pod (bean), split (optional)

a pinch of sea salt (optional)

Marshmallow Fluff

~

This fluff is so buff. It has transformative powers, transporting a boring cup of hot chocolate from 'yawn' to something worthy of going viral. It's the toasted barrier that keeps oozing salted caramel inside Goozey Cookies (see page 99) and the slick of snazziness that will make your popsicles pop (see page 80).

Makes 285 g (10 oz/5 cups)

Measure the sugar, golden syrup and water into a small saucepan and briefly stir to combine.

In the bowl of an electric stand mixer, whisk the egg whites until foamy on a medium speed. With the motor still running, add the cream of tartar and continue to whisk until soft peaks form when you lift the blades out of the mixture.

Now turn your attention to the water mixture. Place the pan over a high heat and bring to 115°C (239°F).

Once the caramel has reached that temperature, remove the pan from the heat and leave for 20 seconds for the bubbling to subside. Then, with the motor running on high, add the hot sugar syrup to the bowl of the mixer, pouring slowly down the inside edge of the bowl to avoid splattering.

Continue to whisk for a few minutes on high until thick and fluffy. The fluff is ready when it starts to clump around the whisk. It may still be warm so leave to cool fully before storing or using.

Store in the fridge in an airtight container for up to 1 week.

90 g (3¼ oz/generous ⅓ cup) caster (superfine) sugar

125 g (4 oz/generous ⅓ cup) golden (light corn) syrup

3 tbsp water

2 medium free-range egg whites

¼ tsp cream of tartar

Brown Butter

If caramelisation – the liquefying and darkening of sugar – is my favourite scientific reaction, Maillard is my second. It occurs when browning butter, giving it its distinctly nutty, toasty smell and flavour profile. The browning becomes noticeable once the water has evaporated at 100°C (212°F), which is when the temperature can increase further and the lactose in the milk solids starts to brown – 'Maillardisation'. The technique in this recipe works for any amount and type of dairy butter; just ensure that you increase the pan size if you increase the quantity of butter. This recipe, as an example, makes the quantity of brown butter required for Caramel Apple Pie Blondies (see page 89). Excess butter can be stored in an ice-cube tray in the freezer for up to two months.

Makes approximately 225 g (8 oz/1 cup)

Put the butter in a large, light-coloured, heavy-based saucepan. The light colour of the pan allows the browning to be clearly seen and the heavy base allows for even heat dispersion and cooking.

Set the pan over a low-medium heat and allow the butter to gently melt, stirring from time to time.

Once melted, the butter will begin to bubble and splatter dramatically. Swirl the pan or gently stir the butter during this stage to calm it and release the boiling bubbles.

Once all the water has evaporated, the butter will begin to foam and the milk solids will begin to brown. Pay close attention and stir often to release the milk solids from the bottom of the pan as they can easily catch and burn. The milk solids will turn from pale gold to deep amber very quickly.

I like to take the butter off the heat halfway through this transformation and allow the heat of the pan to continue the process. I find this is the easiest way to control the browning to my liking. Alternatively, leave the butter on the heat until ready, then immediately pour the browned butter into a heatproof bowl.

Set the bowl over an ice bath and stir to chill the butter. Use immediately or pour into an ice-cube tray and store in the freezer for up to 2 months.

250 g (9 oz/1 cup) cold salted butter, cubed

Snacks

Snacks are the most important
meals of the day – right?

Cornflake Bocaditos

The first time I served these on my market stall at Druid Street in London, people went crazy for them. One wonderful lady used to come prepared with a big plastic tub and buy them all except one that she would leave for the next lucky customer. These are now a Fatties must-have! They are a simple, deeply satisfying snack, sweet with condensed milk and rich with dark, complex caramel and sea salt.

Makes 15–30 bocaditos, depending on size

Cover a flat work surface with a large piece of baking parchment and half fill a small bowl with water.

Measure out the cornflakes into a large bowl. Set to one side.

In a large, heavy-based saucepan, make a very dark dry caramel with the sugar (see page 16). Once smoking and nearing burnt, add the butter and stir to incorporate.

Turn the heat down to low and add the condensed milk. Stir thoroughly to combine and to avoid the condensed milk catching on the bottom of the pan. Add the sea salt and the cornflakes. Gently fold the cornflakes into the caramel, coating each one but being careful not to crush. Remove the pan from the heat and leave to cool slightly until cool enough to handle.

Using number 30 portioner (see page 12) or equivalent, scoop out single mounds for mini bocaditos or double scoops for bigger ones onto the prepared surface, dampening your hands in the water as you go and compressing the heaps to help the mounds stick together.

Leave for about 10 minutes to cool and set fully. Sprinkle with edible glitter or spray with edible shimmer spray paint for a special touch!

Enjoy right away or store in an airtight container for up to 2 days.

200 g (7 oz/6½ cups) cornflakes

225 g (8 oz/1 cup) caster (superfine) sugar

75 g (2½ oz/scant ⅓ cup) salted butter

400 g (14 oz) tinned condensed milk

1 tsp sea salt

edible glitter or edible shimmer spray paint

Robins' Nests

These springtime treats were inspired by the robins nesting in the kitchen window box. We secretly watched them for months, careful not to disturb the nesting pair and eager for the eggs to hatch. Sadly, they never did and the parents eventually abandoned the nest, but in their wake they left behind a real treat. I still think of those robins and wish them success in the future.

Makes 12 nests

Line a 12-hole muffin pan with paper cases. Set to one side.

In a medium bowl, break up the shredded wheat biscuits into strands. Set aside.

In a large, heavy-based saucepan, make a dark dry caramel with the sugar (see page 16). Once smoking, add the butter and stir well to incorporate.

Turn the heat down to low and add the condensed milk. Stir thoroughly to combine and to avoid the condensed milk catching on the bottom of the pan. Add the sea salt and the broken up shredded wheat and stir well, coating every strand. Remove the pan from the heat and leave to cool slightly until cool enough to handle.

Divide the mixture among the cases and, with dampened hands, press out and up the sides to form a nest shape. Leave to set for about 20 minutes.

Meanwhile, melt the chocolate in a small bowl over a pan of gently simmering water, making sure the base of the bowl does not touch the water. Using a pastry brush, paint the insides of the nests with a layer of the melted chocolate. Leave to set.

Once the chocolate has hardened, spoon the caramel sauce into the middle of the nests and fill the nests with mini eggs.

The nests can be stored for 2 days in an airtight container.

8 shredded wheat biscuits (175 g/6 oz)

225 g (8 oz/1 cup) caster (superfine) sugar

75 g (2½ oz/scant ⅓ cup) salted butter

400 g (14 oz) tinned condensed milk

1 tsp sea salt

75 g (2½ oz) good-quality milk or dark chocolate

12 tbsp Classic Salted Caramel Sauce (see page 32), at room temperature

mini chocolate eggs, to decorate

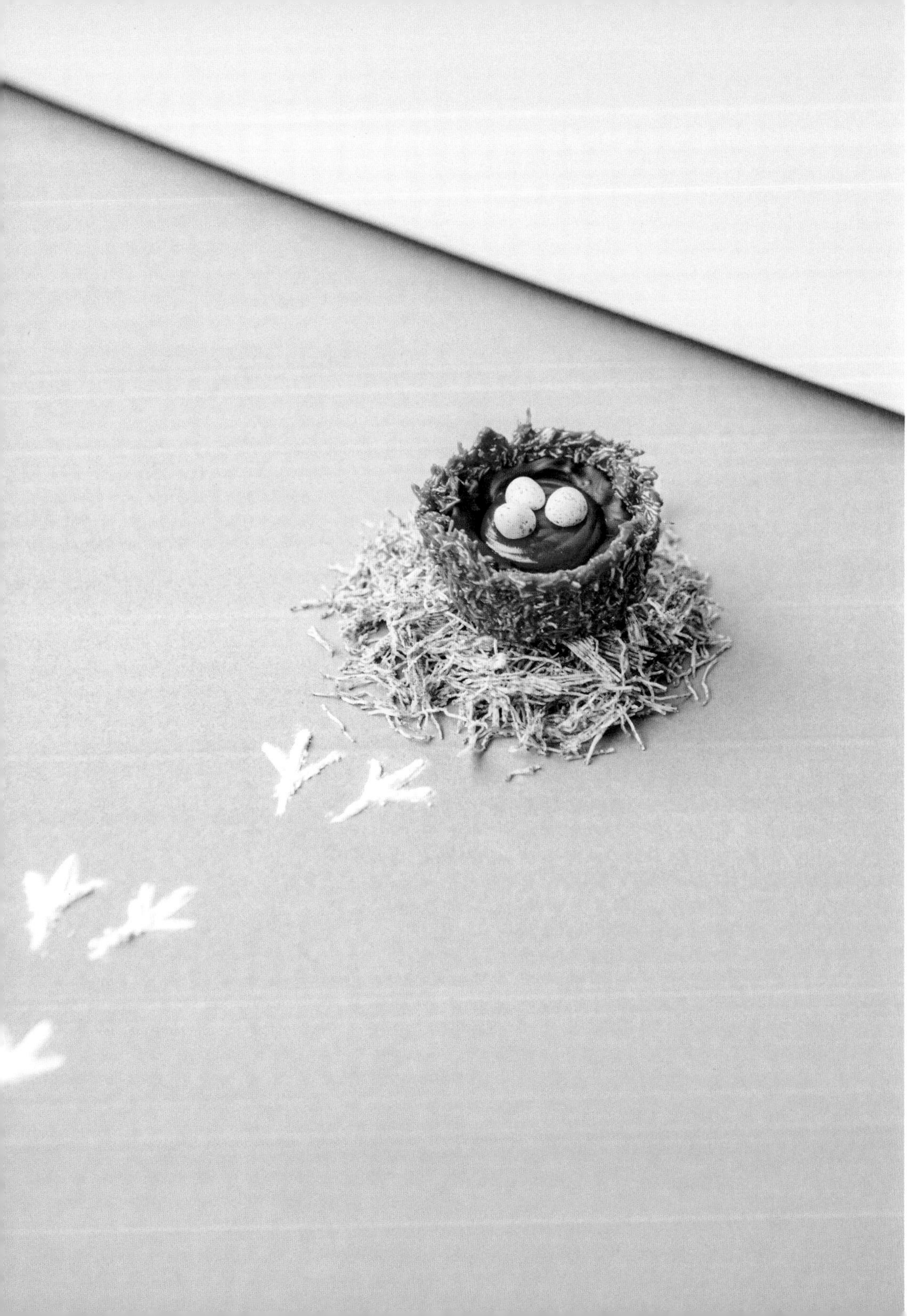

Salted Caramel Peanut Butter

If there's one product that causes a bun fight on my sweet stall it's this, and I don't blame them. People tell me not to give it to them as they know it's a one-way ticket to a one-pot, one-spoon love-in. Here's the recipe, dare to make it or don't …

Natural (organic) peanut butter is prone to separation, so it might need a good stir before you start.

Stir together the peanut butter, salted caramel sauce and sea salt until thoroughly combined.

Store in an airtight container or follow the instructions on sterilising and filling (see page 20).

100 g (3½ oz/scant ½ cup) natural (organic) peanut butter , crunchy or smooth

100 g (3½ oz) Classic Salted Caramel Sauce (see page 32), at room temperature

½ tsp sea salt

Chocolate Chip Salted Caramel Peanut Butter

To make it even more irresistible, add 30 g (1 oz/2 tbsp) good-quality chopped dark chocolate or chocolate chips.

Snacks ~ p.64

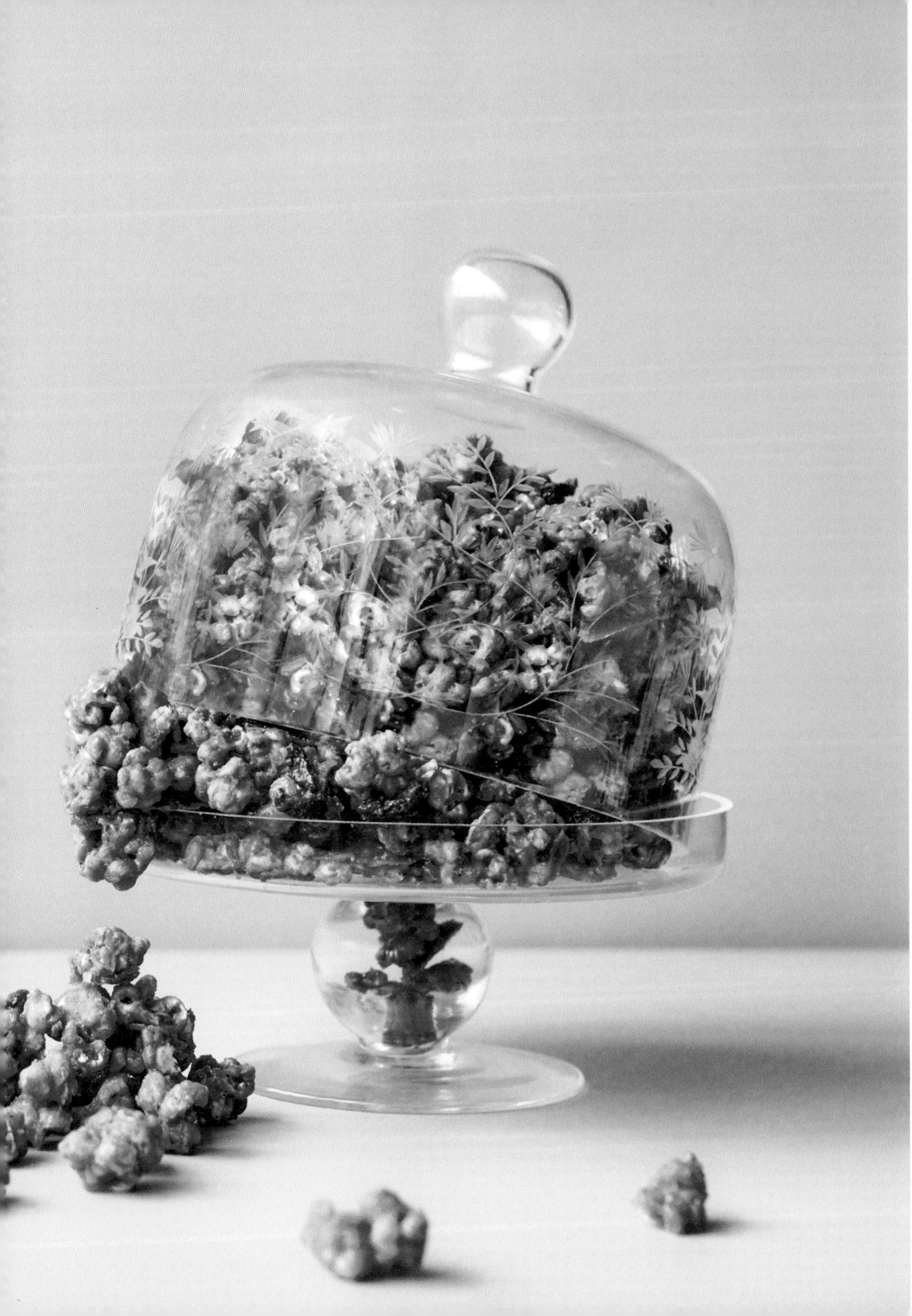

Snacks ~ p.65

Crunchy Maple Bacon Popcorn

I made this popcorn for Meatopia, a festival of meat held in London once a year. By the end of the weekend people were requesting straight-up boxes of the stuff. Like any popcorn, it's totally moreish, but the candied bacon really takes it to another level. For a spicy twist, I like to add a teaspoon of cayenne pepper when whisking in the bicarbonate of soda.

Throw together a couple of scoops of vanilla ice cream, a big spoonful of Bananas Foster Caramel Sauce (see page 43), some Salted Caramel Peanut Butter (see page 62) and a handful of this popcorn and you've got yourself a Fatties Elvis Sundae.

Makes about 500 g (1 lb 2 oz)

Preheat the oven to 120°C (250°F/Gas ½).

In a very large, cold pan, render the bacon over a low heat until the fat has melted and is beginning to foam and the bacon is dark and golden. This should take about 10–15 minutes.

Remove the bacon from the pan with a slotted spoon, reserving the bacon fat, and set to one side in a small bowl.

Add a few popcorn kernels to the pan with the bacon fat and place the pan over a medium-high heat. Once they start popping, add the rest of the kernels, fit the pan with a lid and shake well to coat the popcorn kernels in the fat. Return to the heat and cook until the kernels begin to pop rapidly. Once they do, adjust the lid a little to allow the steam to escape but not the popping corn. As the popping sounds subside to a few seconds apart, remove the pan from the heat and allow the heat of the pan to finish the job.

Pour the popped popcorn into a large bowl, discarding any unpopped kernels. Toss the bacon into the popcorn and divide between 2 large, non-stick, rimmed baking sheets.

In a clean, medium saucepan, melt together the butter, brown sugar, golden syrup and maple syrup over a low heat, stirring continuously. Bring to a simmer, then cook for 2 minutes, stirring occasionally. After 2 minutes, remove from the heat and whisk in the bicarbonate of soda.

Immediately pour the mixture over the popcorn, dividing it between the 2 baking sheets. Stir the popcorn to coat in the hot caramel, but don't worry if every kernel isn't covered – it will all be incorporated as you continue to stir through the baking process.

Bake for 45 minutes–1 hour, stirring every 15 minutes. To check the development, take out a piece of popcorn at the 45 minute stage and leave it to cool, then taste it to see if it is crunchy enough. If not, continue cooking, repeating the process every 5 minutes.

Once you are happy, remove the popcorn from the oven and leave to cool on the baking sheets for a few minutes. Spread a large sheet of baking parchment over a flat work surface, then use a large spatula to transfer the popcorn to the paper and leave to cool.

Popcorn can be stored for up to 1 week in an airtight container at room temperature.

400 g (14 oz) smoked bacon or pancetta lardons, chopped

150 g (5 oz/⅔ cup) unpopped popcorn kernels

225 g (8 oz/scant 1 cup) salted butter

450 g (1 lb/2¼ cups) soft light brown sugar

125 g (4 oz/generous ⅓ cup) golden (light corn) syrup

50 ml (2 fl oz/¼ cup) maple syrup

½ tsp bicarbonate of soda (baking soda)

Malted Mallows

Puffy and fluffy, these marshmallows are a sweet, comforting confection, reminiscent of malted milkshakes and nights by the campfire.

Makes 24 marshmallows

To make the malted caramel, make a wet caramel with the sugar, golden syrup and water (see page 18). Cook to a medium colour before adding the cream, sea salt and malt syrup. Stir to a smooth caramel. Set to one side.

To make the vanilla mallows, mix the gelatine with two-thirds of the water in a mug or small bowl, and soak for 5 minutes. Microwave until the gelatine has dissolved, whisking until smooth. Add to the bowl of a stand mixer fitted with the whisk along with half of the golden syrup. Leave running on slow. Put the remaining golden syrup, the remaining water and the sugar in a small saucepan and heat over a medium heat, without stirring, to 115°C (239°F). Slowly stream it into the stand mixer and beat for 5 minutes on low, then 5 minutes on medium and 5 minutes on high until thick, pure white and opaque.

While the marshmallow is whipping, grease a 20 cm (8 in) square cake tin or silicone mould.

To make the dusting powder, sift together the ingredients into a large bowl. Once combined, sprinkle the prepared cake tin with enough powder to form an even layer. Set to one side, reserving the remaining powder.

Whisk the vanilla extract into the whipped marshmallow and remove the whisk, scraping it down well as the marshmallow will stick. Add the caramel and marble through with a large spatula but do not overmix. Pour the ribboned mixture into the prepared cake tin, smoothing the top with the spatula. Sprinkle over enough dusting powder to cover (reserving some for later). Leave to set at room temperature for 6–8 hours.

Dust a work surface with some of the reserved powder. Gently run a knife around the sides of the marshmallow and turn it out. Slice into 24 pieces using a sharp knife. Place the bowl of dusting powder, then toss well to coat completely.

Remove the marshmallows from the powder and store in an airtight container at room temperature for up to 1 week. The marshmallows may weep slightly after a few days, but a quick dip in more dusting powder will fix that.

Malted caramel swirl

75 g (2½ oz/⅓ cup) caster (superfine) sugar

1 tbsp golden (light corn) syrup

2 tbsp water

80 ml (2½ fl oz/⅓ cup) double (heavy) cream, at room temperature

½ tsp sea salt

1 tbsp malt syrup

Vanilla mallows

5 tsp gelatine

185 ml (6½fl oz/¾ cup) water, divided into two-thirds and one-third

200 g (7oz/generous ½ cup) golden (light corn) syrup, divided in half

175 g (6oz/¾ cup) caster (superfine) sugar

a little butter, for greasing

1 tsp vanilla extract

Dusting powder

75 g (2½ oz/scant ⅔ cup) icing (confectioners') sugar

50 g (2 oz/scant ½ cup) cornflour (cornstarch)

25 g (1oz/¼ cup) malted milk powder

Golden Macaroons

A twist on a classic Scottish coconut macaroon (not to be confused with the fancy French macaron), these unassuming coconut haystacks hide a deeply caramelised interior. The sweetness of a traditional macaroon is swept away with the use of caramel sugar and a good pinch of sea salt. In the words of my friend Cat, 'They are so luxury'.

Makes 14–15 macaroons, depending on scoop size

Combine all the ingredients (except the extra desiccated coconut) in a large pan. Stir well to combine.

Cook over a medium-low heat for about 5 minutes, stirring often, until the mixture becomes porridgy and loose. Turn up the heat to medium and continue to cook for a further 5–8 minutes, stirring constantly, until the mixture thickens and the bottom starts to sizzle. When ready, the mixture should hold together in a clump when pressed to the side of the pan.

Leave to cool in the pan until the mixture is cool enough to handle. Stir from time to time to assist the cooling and avoid a dry crust forming.

While the macaroon mix is cooling, preheat the oven to 160°C (320°F/Gas 3), pour the remaining desiccated coconut into a small bowl and line a large baking sheet with baking parchment.

When ready, scoop out the mix with a number 16 portioner or with dampened hands to form mounds about the size of 3 tablespoons. Roll in the coconut until evenly coated, and place on the prepared baking sheet.

Bake for 15–18 minutes or until golden brown and toasty.

Leave to cool on the baking sheet for 10 minutes before removing to a wire rack to cool fully.

Decorate as desired! I like to top mine with caramel sauce.

375 g (13 oz/1⅔ cups) Caramel Sugar (see page 44)

6 large free-range egg whites

1 tsp sea salt

300 g (10½ oz/3⅓ cup) unsweetened desiccated (shredded) coconut plus 75 g (2½ oz/generous ¾ cup) for rolling

Classic Salted Caramel Sauce (see page 32), to top, (optional)

Caramel Rye Truffles

Makes 20 truffles

I love these truffles with the added crunch of the dehydrated rye bread, but feel free to leave it out. They may not look all that pretty as little rocky brown boulders, but once tasted, you'll soon fall for them.

100 g (3½ oz) German-style rye bread

75 g (2½ oz/scant ⅓ cup) caster (superfine) sugar

150 ml (5 fl oz/scant ⅔ cup) double (heavy) cream

½ tsp sea salt

225 g (8 oz) dark chocolate with at least 70% cocoa

25 g (1 oz/scant ¼ cup) cocoa (unsweetened chocolate) powder

Preheat the oven to 100°C (212°F/Gas ¼) or its lowest setting.

Begin by dehydrating the rye bread. Finely crumble the rye bread and spread over a large baking sheet. Bake for 30 minutes, or until no moisture remains and the crumbs are light and crunchy but not browned. Stir the crumbs from time to time to ensure even cooking. Set the rye crumbs aside to cool as you make the truffle mix.

In a small, heavy-based saucepan, make a dark dry caramel with the sugar (see page 16). Remove from the heat and stir in the cream and sea salt, watching out for hot splashing. Set aside to cool as you continue to the next step. The caramel should be just warm to the touch when ready to be used.

Melt the chocolate in a medium-sized heatproof bowl set over a pan of gently simmering water, making sure the bottom of the bowl does not touch the water. Stir until just melted but not hot. Alternatively, melt gently in the microwave in a suitable container. Add the cooled caramel to the melted chocolate and stir well. Add the rye crumbs and mix again.

Leave the truffle mix, uncovered, for about 30 minutes at room temperature to firm up slightly. Give the mixture a stir from time to time to make sure it sets evenly, especially around the edges of the bowl.

Line a baking sheet with baking parchment, scoop out tablespoons of the truffle and place on the prepared sheet. Leave for 20-40 minutes to set fully. It should be firm to the touch.

Measure the cocoa into a large resealable freezer bag, add the truffles and shake well to coat the truffles.

The truffles will keep for 2 weeks at room temperature in an airtight container or up to 1 month in the fridge.

Snacks ~ p.72

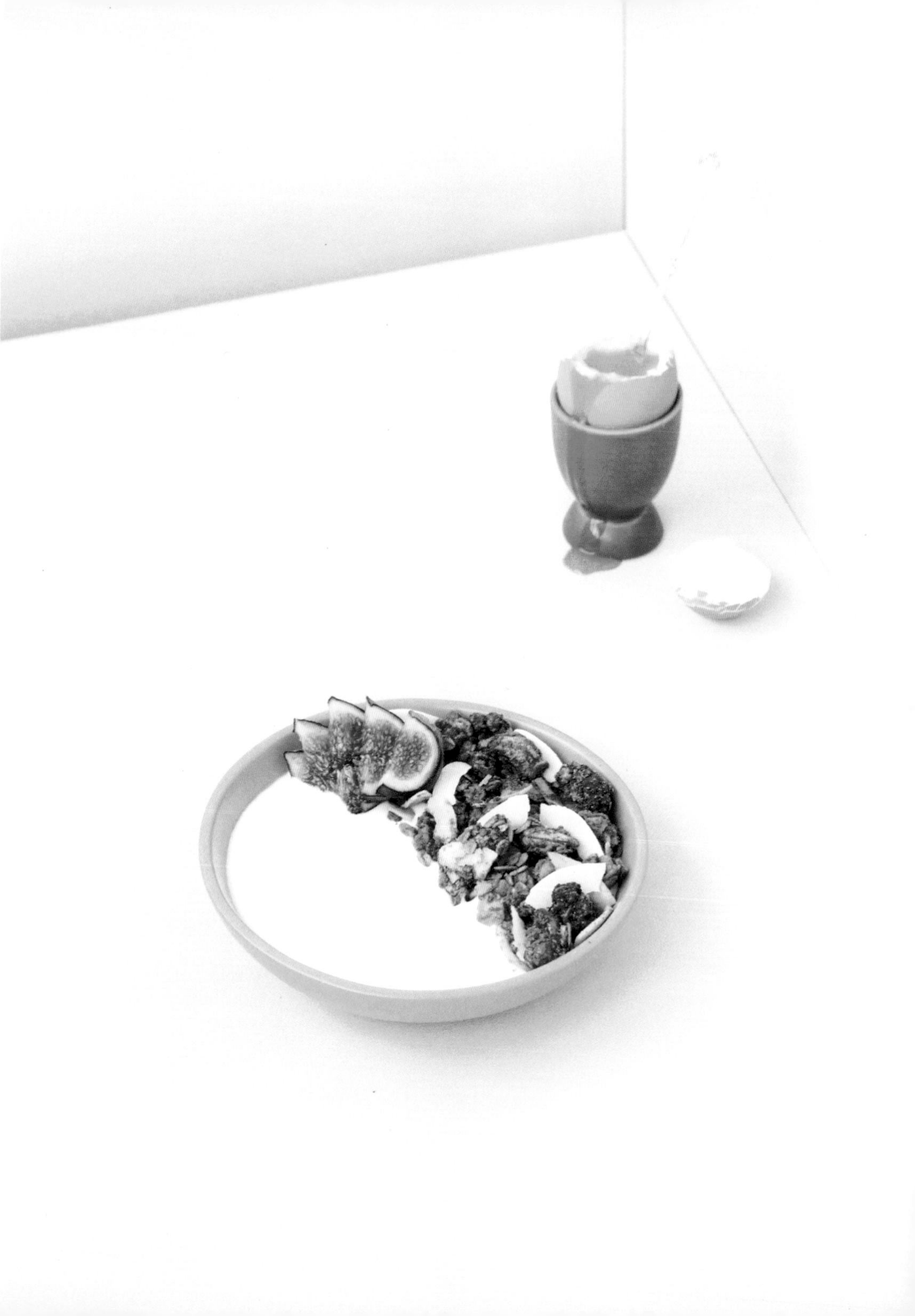

Fatties' Favourite Granola

Makes 900 g (2 lb) jar

I really wanted an indulgent granola recipe in this book and I knew just the person to turn to. Enter Rebecca from Rock My Bowl, the maker of the best granola in London. This recipe is lovely served with yoghurt and fruit for breakfast and makes a great dessert served with mascarpone and warm honey.

275 g (10 oz/2¾ cups) jumbo rolled oats

250 g (9 oz/1 cup) coconut oil

100 ml (3½ fl oz/scant ½ cup) date syrup, divided into 5 tbsp and 2 tbsp

1 tsp vanilla extract

200 g (7 oz/scant 1 cup) Salted Caramel Peanut Butter (see page 62), at room temperature

30 g (1 oz/2 tbsp) coconut sugar (or any brown sugar will work)

125 g (4 oz/generous ¾ cup) cashew nuts, roughly chopped

75 g (2½ oz/1¼ cups) coconut flakes

Preheat the oven to 160°C (325°F/Gas 3) and line a large baking sheet with baking parchment.

Measure the oats into a large mixing bowl. Gently melt the coconut oil in a small saucepan over a low heat, then add the 5 tablespoons of date syrup and the vanilla extract. Stir well to combine before adding to the oats and giving it another mix.

In the same pan in which you melted the coconut oil, gently melt the salted caramel peanut butter until warm, keeping a close eye on it and stirring often to stop it catching. Stir the melted peanut butter into the oat mixture. When thoroughly combined, pour into the prepared baking sheet and press down firmly so it's compact. Bake for 20 minutes, then carefully rotate the tray. Bake for a further 10 minutes, turn again and bake for a final 10 minutes.

While the granola is baking, melt the additional 2 tablespoons of date syrup with the coconut sugar in a frying pan (skillet). Add the cashews and coconut flakes and heat over a low heat for about 5 minutes until they are caramelised.

After the last 10 minutes of baking, add the cashews and coconut to the top of the granola, but don't mix! Turn up the oven temperature to 180°C (350°F/Gas 4) and bake for a further 10 minutes.

Turn the oven off and open the door. Ideally, you want to leave the granola to cool in the oven. However, if you just can't wait to dig in, place the granola on a cooling rack and cool for 30 minutes–1 hour. Your granola will be in large clusters.

Give the granola a bash to break it up slightly, then mix through the cashews and coconut.

Store in an airtight container at room temperature for up to 6 weeks.

Snacks ~ p.75

Dippy Brioche Doughnuts

Being a child of split parents meant that I spent some of my early years frequenting motorway service stop cafés. Eating tiny doughnuts dipped in chocolate sauce is one of my strongest memories of these times. I still find them such a simply comforting pleasure. I've put a Fatties twist on the chocolate sauce with a base of dark salty caramel and the brioche doughnuts are light and fluffy unlike the greasy ones of my youth. See photo on previous page.

Makes approximately
18-20 doughnuts

In the bowl of a stand mixer, mix together the flour, salt, sugar and yeast with a hand whisk.

Warm the milk in a small saucepan, over a low-medium heat or in the microwave in a small jug, until just warm to the touch. Add the warmed milk to the dry ingredients along with the eggs and egg yolk. Stir together briefly with a spatula or wooden spoon.

Fit the mixer with the dough hook and mix on a low-medium speed until smooth.

Add the softened butter, cube by cube, kneading in the butter for a further 6 minutes or until it is fully incorporated.

Increase the speed to medium-high and knead for an additional 6 minutes or until a sticky but glossy dough is formed.

Oil a medium bowl. Transfer the dough to the bowl, cover with oiled cling film (plastic wrap) and refrigerate overnight to prove for up to 12 hours. The dough will not quite double in size but will be larger.

In the morning, remove the dough from the fridge. Lightly sprinkle a work surface with flour, tip out the dough onto the pre-pared surface, scraping it from the bottom of the bowl. Dust a little more flour on top and roll out to a thickness of 1 cm (½ in). Using a 5 cm (2 in) round cutter, stamp out as many circles as you can. Using your index finger, poke a little hole in the middle of each of the dough circles, spinning out to a larger hole as you

250 g (9 oz/2 cups) strong white bread flour, plus extra for dusting

¼ tsp fine sea salt

25 g (1 oz/2 tbsp) caster (superfine) sugar

7 g (¼ oz/1 sachet) fast-action dried yeast

75 ml (2½ fl oz/⅓ cup) full-fat (whole) milk

2 large free-range eggs, at room temperature

1 large free-range egg yolk, at room temperature

115 g (3¾ oz/½ cup) very soft unsalted butter, cubed

2 litres (70 fl oz/8 cups) sunflower oil, for frying, plus extra for greasing

75 g caster (superfine) sugar for dredging

1 tsp ground cinnamon (optional)

would making a bagel. Lightly flour a large baking sheet and place the doughnuts on it, leaving space between for them to double in size. Cover lightly with cling film and leave to rise for 1 hour, or until doubled in size.

As the doughnuts near the end of their second prove, heat the oil in a large saucepan or deep fat fryer to 180°C (350°F).

In a medium bowl, whisk the sugar with the cinnamon, if using. Layer some paper towels on a work surface to drain the doughnuts on as they come out of the fryer.

Fry the doughnuts in batches of 4. Very gently lower the doughnuts into the hot oil. They should puff up and float. Turn them over in the oil, frying for a few minutes on each side, or until puffed and golden. If proved correctly, the doughnuts should have a pale 'proof line' around the middle. Remove the doughnuts with a slotted spoon and drain on the paper before tossing in the sugar and cinnamon mix. Repeat until all the doughnuts have been fried and sugar coated.

Serve immediately while warm, with the hot chocolate dip (see below).

Salted Caramel Hot Chocolate Dip

Makes 1 very generous bowlful

This sauce makes the perfect dip for the doughnuts (see above) but is just as good used as a glaze. Any leftover sauce is fantastic with ice cream.

100 g (3½ oz/scant ½ cup) caster (superfine) sugar

200 ml (7 fl oz/generous ¾ cup) whipping cream, at room temperature

200 g (7 oz) good-quality dark chocolate, broken into chunks

25 g (1 oz/2 tbsp) salted butter

1 tsp sea salt

50 ml (2 fl oz/¼ cup) boiling water

In a medium, heavy-based saucepan, make a dark dry caramel with the sugar (see page 16). Slowly add the cream to the pan, stirring only once the bubbling has subsided. Stir well to melt the caramel into the cream.

Remove the pan from the heat and whisk in the chocolate, followed by the butter, sea salt and finally the boiling water.

Serve warm or store in the fridge for up to 1 week. To serve, simply melt in the microwave in short bursts or in a small pan over a low heat, stirring often.

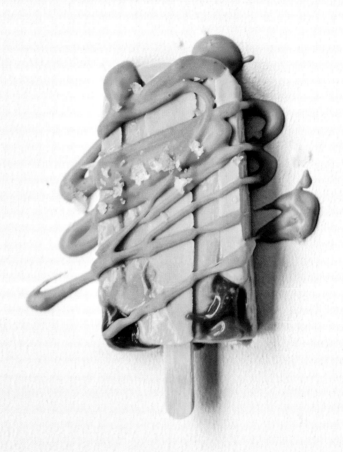

Caramel Popcorn Pop, see page 81

Hot Choc Pop, see page 80

Hot Choc Pop

In high summer, I love eating cookies and chunks of frozen brownie cold and chewy from the fridge. Taking that inspiration, I've updated my ever-popular salted caramel and marshmallow hot chocolate, giving it a cool, cooling makeover. See photo on page 79.

In a medium saucepan, bring the milk and cream to a gentle simmer. Remove the pan from the heat and add the chocolate, sugar and vanilla extract, then stir well until smooth and well combined. Pour into a jug and leave to cool, whisking from time to time to aid cooling. The faster you can bring the temperature down, the better. Sprinkle in the sea salt and stir once more.

Once cool, pour into lolly (popsicle) moulds, pop in the sticks and refrigerate until cold. Once cold, move to the freezer and freeze for 6–8 hours until set. Chilling the mixture before freezing makes for extra-creamy pops.

Once frozen, remove the ice pops from the moulds by running under lukewarm water for a few seconds and gently releasing. Ice pops can be stored, un-moulded, in a freezer bag for 1 month.

For the full Fatties experience, just before serving, drizzle over some caramel sauce, pipe some marshmallow fluff on top, and blowtorch!

Makes 8 × 85 ml (3 fl oz) lollies, depending on your mould capacity

350 ml (12 fl oz/1½ cups) full-fat (whole) milk

170 ml (6 fl oz/⅔ cup) double (heavy) cream

100 g (3½ oz) good-quality dark chocolate, finely chopped

35 g (1¼ oz/2½ tbsp) caster (superfine) sugar

1 tsp vanilla extract

½ tsp sea salt

To serve

Classic Salted Caramel Sauce (see page 32), at room temperature

Marshmallow Fluff (see page 52)

Caramel Popcorn Pop

Makes 8 × 85 ml (3 fl oz) lollies, depending on your mould capacity

A delicious pop, flecked with smoky salted caramel and flavoured with popcorn. Perfect for movie night. See photo on page 78.

Base

2 tbsp popcorn kernels

1 tsp sunflower oil

400 ml (14 fl oz/generous 1½ cups) full-fat (whole) milk

200 ml (7 fl oz/generous ¾ cup) double (heavy) cream

15 g (½ oz/1 tbsp) cornflour (cornstarch)

100 g (3½ oz/generous ½ cup) soft light brown sugar

½ tsp smoked sea salt

Caramel ripple

50 g (2 oz/scant ¼ cup) caster (superfine) sugar

60 ml (2 fl oz/¼ cup) double (heavy) cream

½ tsp smoked sea salt

To serve

Caramelised White Chocolate (see page 46), melted

In a medium pan fitted with a lid, cook the popcorn kernels in the sunflower oil, until they have all popped. Add the milk and cream and simmer over a low heat, stirring well, without allowing the mixture to boil. Remove from the heat and leave to steep for 1 hour.

Once infused, strain the milk and cream mixture into a clean saucepan, discarding the popcorn. Warm the mixture again over a low heat until the mixture begins to simmer, then remove from the heat.

Measure out the cornflour into a small heatproof bowl. Pour 4 tablespoons of the warm milk mixture into the cornflour, whisking well until you have a smooth paste and no lumps remain.

Add the brown sugar and sea salt to the remaining milk mixture, whisking to dissolve, then bring back up to a simmer. Turn off the heat and add the cornflour mix, whisking all the time. Return the pan to a low-medium heat and cook, still whisking, for 3–5 minutes until the mixture is the consistency of a thin custard.

Remove from the heat and strain the mixture into a jug. Leave to cool to room temperature, whisking from time to time to aid the cooling. The faster you can bring the temperature down, the better. Once cool, place in the fridge to chill completely.

Make the caramel ripple. In a small, heavy-based saucepan, make a dark dry caramel with the sugar (see page 16). Remove from the heat then add the cream, watching out for steam and splatters. Once the bubbling has subsided, add the sea salt and stir to a smooth consistency. Leave to cool to room temperature.

Once the base mix is chilled and the caramel is cool, ripple the caramel into the jug (you will get nice big flecks). Divide the mixture between the lolly (popsicle) moulds, pop in the sticks and freeze for 6–8 hours until set.

Once frozen, remove the ice pops from the moulds by running under lukewarm water for a few seconds and gently releasing. Ice pops can be stored, un-moulded in a freezer bag for 1 month.

For a delicious finish, drizzle the ice pops with a little caramelised white chocolate.

Brownies, Bars + Cookies

Grab your pickaxe, we're going
mining for gold…

The Goldmine Brownie

This is the 'Ohh, baby' of all my brownies, the one
that has you tripping over your heels for a piece.
The sign on my stall reads 'Get one and you'll
understand', but to go into a little more detail,
this is a truly seductive dark chocolate brownie,
intensified with coffee and lit with cinnamon.
Oh and yes, the canyons and rivers of caramel ...

Makes 16 brownies

Preheat the oven to 170°C (350°F/Gas 4). Butter and line a
30 × 20 cm (12 × 8 in) brownie pan with baking parchment.

Sift the flour into a bowl and add the sea salt. In a separate bowl,
whisk together the cocoa and espresso powders. Weigh out the
sugar in another bowl and the chocolate chips in another.

Gently melt the butter in a large saucepan over a medium heat.
Remove the from the heat and, using a rubber spatula, gently mix
in the cocoa and espresso powders and stir to a smooth paste.

Add the sugar in three stages, mixing thoroughly but gently to
obtain a thick paste. Add the eggs two at a time, beating well but
not vigorously so you incorporate as little air into the mix as
possible. Fold through the flour and salt mix and then the
chocolate chips, until throughly combined.

Pour two-thirds of the brownie batter into the prepared brownie
pan and smooth to form an even layer. Dollop the cold salted
caramel over the top. The larger the dollops, the more extreme the
pockets of caramel in the finished brownies – if they are smaller,
you'll get a more uniform layer. Working quickly before the mixture cools and seizes, ripple over the remaining one-third of the
brownie batter to cover the entire surface of the previous layers.

Bake for 20–25 minutes, or until firm around the edges but still
slightly jiggly in the middle.

Leave to cool in the pan, then refrigerate for at least 4 hours before
cutting. Brownies are best stored in the fridge for up to 1 week.

350 g (12 oz/generous
1⅓ cups) salted butter,
plus extra for greasing

115 g (3¾ oz/generous ¾ cup)
plain (all-purpose) flour

1 tsp sea salt

200 g (7 oz/scant 2 cups)
cocoa (unsweetened
chocolate) powder

2 tbsp instant espresso
powder

650 g (1 lb 7 oz/scant 3 cups)
caster (superfine) sugar

6 large free-range eggs

200 g (7 oz/1¼ cups) good-
quality dark chocolate chips

300 g (10½ oz) Classic Salted
Caramel Sauce (see page 32),
chilled

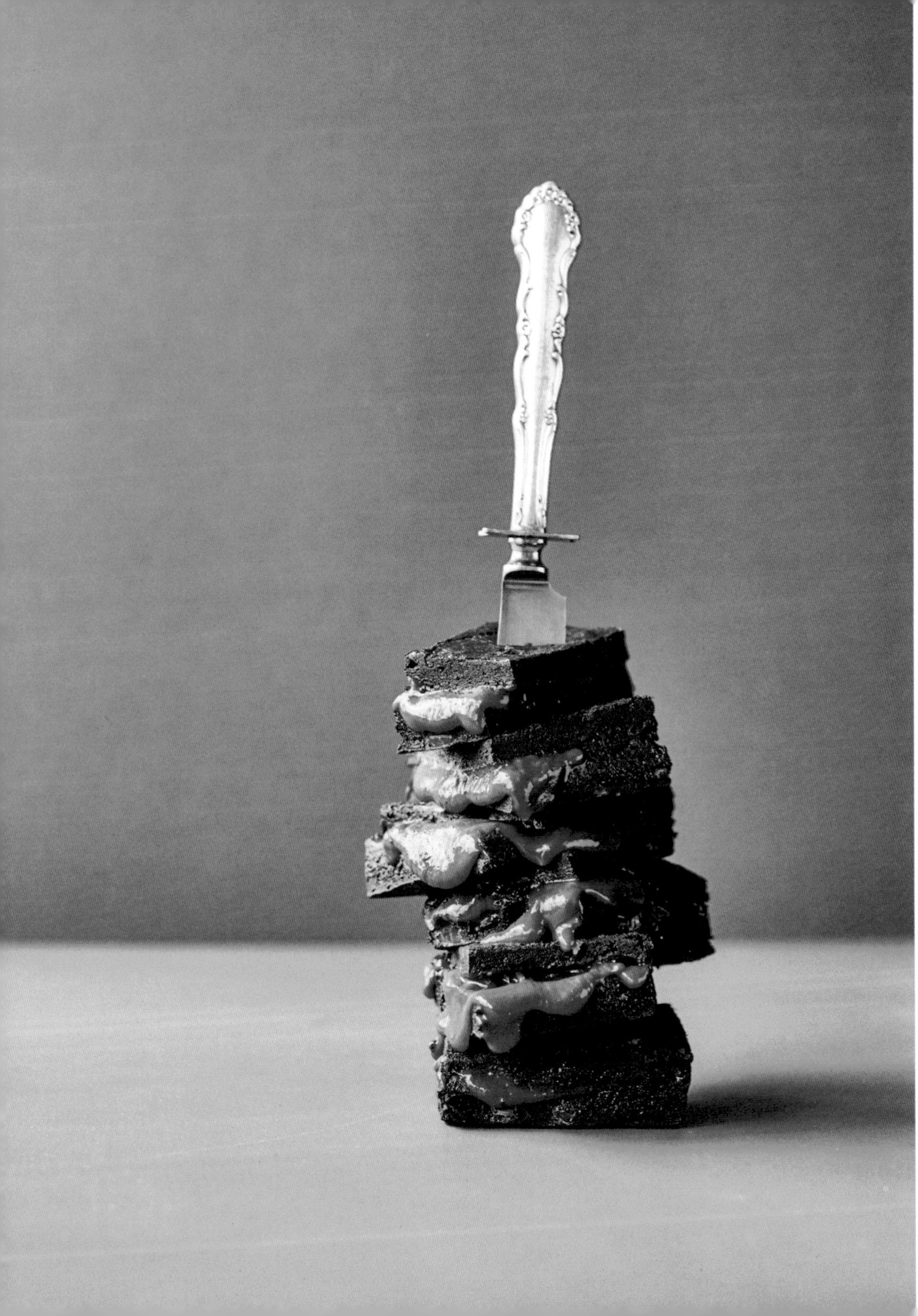

Coconut Flour Brownies

These were the brownies that made me fall in love with brownies. Before I came up with this recipe, I hated them. I know, right – weird. I'm a changed woman and this recipe will always remain close to my heart. These are light but still deliciously fudgy. Magically, they are also gluten free!

Makes 8 brownies

Preheat the oven to 180°C (350°F/Gas 4). Grease and line a 20 cm (8 in) square brownie pan or silicone mould.

Melt the butter in a medium saucepan over a gentle heat. Once only a small lump of unmelted butter remains, remove the pan from the heat and swirl the pan until all of the butter has melted. Doing it this way stops the butter from getting too hot.

Vigorously beat the sugar and cocoa into the melted butter. Don't panic if the mixture looks grainy. The mixture should be warm to the touch but not hot. If you can't comfortably hold your finger in the mix for more than 5 seconds, leave it to cool until you can.

Add the eggs all at once and beat until fully incorporated and you have a smooth and glossy mixture. Sift the coconut flour into the batter. Beat in well, checking for pockets of flour and breaking them up. Stir in the sea salt.

Pour the mixture into the prepared pan, wiggle the pan to smooth the top and tap on the work surface a few times to get rid of air pockets. Drizzle over the warmed caramel sauce and scatter over the chocolate chips. Bake for 20–25 minutes or until just a small jiggle remains in the middle.

Cool the brownies in the pan on a wire rack. Once cooled to room temperature, place in the fridge. Chill for at least 1 hour before cutting so that you get neat slices. Brownies are best stored in the fridge for up to 1 week.

140 g (4½ oz/scant ⅔ cup) cold salted butter, cubed, plus extra to grease

250 g (9 oz/generous 1 cup) caster (superfine) sugar

65 g (2¼ oz/generous ½ cup) cocoa (unsweetened chocolate) powder

3 large free-range eggs

35 g (1¼ oz/generous ¼ cup) coconut flour

1 tsp good flakey sea salt

150 g (5 oz) Classic Salted Caramel Sauce (see page 32), warmed to a liquid

50 g (2 oz/⅓ cup) good dark chocolate chips or chopped chocolate

Additions and alternatives

Replace the Classic Salted Caramel Sauce with any of the sauce recipes in this book.

Add some Salted Caramel Peanut Butter (page 62) and chunks of milk chocolate.

Add some Caramelised White Chocolate (page 46), as pictured, and a handful of toasted hazelnuts.

Brownies, Bars + Cookies ~ p.87

Fondant Brownies

Seemingly unassuming, these brownies hide a heart of gold – split them open and your heart will melt too. Keep a batch of these in your freezer and you can have an indulgent dessert ready in just 15 minutes with nothing more complicated than turning on the oven.

Makes 12 brownies

Preheat the oven to 180°C (350°F/Gas 4). Line the middle oven rack with kitchen foil to catch any run-over caramel and stop it burning to the bottom of the oven.

Melt the 2 tablespoons of butter in a small saucepan, then, using a pastry brush, paint the inside of the cups of a 12-hole muffin pan.

In a large bowl, whisk together the sugar and cocoa powder. Set to one side, but keep close at hand.

In a large saucepan, brown the remaining butter (see page 54).

Once the butter is golden brown and smelling wonderfully nutty, immediately add the cocoa and sugar mix, the water and sea salt. Mix well and quickly to stop the cocoa from catching on the bottom of the hot pan. Leave to cool until the mixture is just warm to the touch before beating in the eggs 2 at a time. Sift over the flour and beat it in quickly with a rubber spatula or wooden spoon.

Fill each prepared muffin cup two-thirds full with the brownie batter. Position a teaspoon of the cold salted caramel sauce in the middle of each brownie.

Bake for 12 minutes until puffed and the caramel is bubbling.

Cover a cooling rack with baking parchment. If any of the brownies burst their bottoms, the paper will stop the warm caramel dripping out.

Leave the brownies to cool on the baking sheet until warm but no longer hot to the touch. To remove the brownies, run an offset spatula around the top of each brownie to gently loosen it from the pan, then lift each one out onto the lined cooling rack.

Serve straight away or leave to cool completely before freezing ready to be enjoyed another day.

To reheat from frozen, place the brownies on a baking sheet lined with baking parchment. Bake at 160°C (325°F/Gas 3) for 15 minutes or until the caramel is bubbling. Serve immediately.

300 g (10½ oz/1¼ cups) salted butter, plus 2 tbsp for greasing

400 g (14 oz/generous 1¾ cups) caster (superfine) sugar

140 g (4½ oz/1¼ cups) cocoa (unsweetened chocolate) powder

2 tbsp water

1 tsp sea salt

4 large free-range eggs

80 g (3 oz/½ cup) plain (all-purpose) flour

12 tsp Classic Salted Caramel Sauce (see page 32), fridge cold

Caramel Apple Pie Blondies

Makes 16 blondies

Brown butter-flecked batter meets tangy spiced apples, dark salty caramel and crunchy oaty cookies in a blondie fit for a cosy autumn afternoon. I wouldn't judge you if you ate these warm with custard straight from the pan!

Spiced apples

350–400 g (12–14 oz) cooking apples, such as Bramleys

2 tbsp dark rum (optional)

½ tbsp lemon juice

½ tsp ground cinnamon

¼ tsp grated nutmeg

Brown butter blondie batter

250 g (9 oz/generous 1 cup) salted butter, plus extra for greasing

250 g (9 oz/1⅔ cups) plain (all-purpose) flour

1 tsp baking powder

1 tsp sea salt

2 large free-range eggs, at room temperature

1 tsp vanilla extract

250 g (9 oz/1¼ cups) soft light brown sugar

4 digestive biscuits (graham crackers), or similar, broken into pieces

200 g (7 oz) Classic Salted Caramel Sauce (see page 32), warmed to a liquid

Peel, core and roughly chop the apples; small and big pieces are ok. Add to a medium pan with the rest of the spiced apple ingredients. Cook over a medium heat for 5–8 minutes until softened and some of the apples have broken down but not all. Remove from the heat and leave to cool to room temperature.

Preheat the oven to 140°C (275°F/Gas 1). Butter and line a 30 × 20 cm (12 × 8 in) baking tin with baking parchment.

In a large pan, brown the butter (see page 54). Set aside to cool slightly.

In a medium bowl, whisk together the flour, baking powder and sea salt. Set to one side.

In the bowl of a stand mixer fitted with the whisk attachment, or by hand in a large bowl, whisk the eggs, vanilla extract and brown sugar until foamy, pale and thick.

With the mixer running on low, stream in the browned butter. Once added, briefly turn up the speed of the mixer to high to fully amalgamate the butter with the eggs and sugar.

Tip in the dry ingredients, mix slowly to just incorporate, then once again briefly mix on high to fully incorporate. Be very careful not to overmix.

Scoop the batter into the prepared tin and smooth to an even layer with an offset spatula. Dollop over the cooled apples, arrange the broken biscuits on top and finally pour over the caramel. Bake for 35–45 minutes, depending on how gooey you like them. As a rule, the edges should be crunchy and golden with the middle still having a little wobble.

Leave to cool in the baking sheet. For a neat slice, chill in the fridge for 1 hour before cutting.

Store in an airtight container in the fridge for up to 3 days.

Anzac Crumble Bars

Inspired by my Australian friend, Elle, these bars have all the delicious flavours of a classic Anzac biscuit but with a comforting layer of thick salted caramel, sweet coconut macaroon and oaty crumble. I hope I've done her proud!

Preheat the oven to 160°C (325°F/Gas 3). Butter and line a 30 × 20 cm (12 × 8 in) baking tin with baking parchment.

Measure out both types of oats, desiccated coconut, bicarbonate of soda, plain flour, brown sugar and sea salt into a large bowl. Whisk together with a fork to combine, breaking up any sugar clumps as you go, then set to one side.

In a small saucepan over a low heat, melt together the golden syrup and butter. Pour over the dry ingredients and bring together with the fork to form a soft crumble. Spoon two-thirds of the mixture into the bottom of the prepared pan, press down and smooth to an even layer. Reserve the remaining third for topping later.

Bake for 10-12 minutes, or until just golden and slightly puffed. Remove from the oven and leave to cool in the pan while you make the caramel filling and macaroon topping.

In a medium bowl, mix the salted caramel sauce with the flour to form a thick paste. Set to one side.

To make the macaroon topping, combine all the ingredients in a small saucepan. Cook over a low heat, stirring often, until the mixture is loosened. Continue to cook until the mixture thickens again and clumps when pressed to the side of the pan. Stir often to avoid scorching. Remove from the heat and set to one side.

Once the base has cooled, spread over the caramel paste using a small offset spatula to form an even layer, leaving a 2.5 cm (1 in) border from the edge of the pan.

Using a pair of teaspoons, dollop out mounds of the macaroon mixture, almost covering all of the caramel. Sprinkle over the remaining third of the crumble and return the pan to the oven for 15 minutes, or until the top is golden and the caramel almost set.

Remove from the oven and leave to cool in the pan on a cooling rack. Once completely cool, gently remove from the pan and slice into 12 pieces.

Store in an airtight container for up to 3 days.

Base and crumble top

175 g (6 oz/¾ cup) salted butter, plus extra for greasing

50 g (2 oz/½ cup) jumbo rolled oats

50 g (2 oz/½ cup) instant oats (oatmeal)

50 g (2 oz/generous ½ cup) desiccated (dried shredded) coconut

½ tsp bicarbonate of soda (baking soda)

225 g (8 oz/1½ cups) plain (all-purpose) flour

100 g (3½ oz/generous ½ cup) soft light brown sugar

1 tsp sea salt

75 g (2½ oz/scant ¼ cup) golden (light corn) syrup

Caramel filling

350 g (12 oz) Classic Salted Caramel Sauce (see page 32), at room temperature

40 g (1½ oz/generous ¼ cup) plain (all-purpose) flour

Macaroon topping

100 g (3½ oz/generous 1 cup) desiccated (dried shredded) coconut

100 g (3½ oz/scant ½ cup) caster (superfine) sugar

2 large free-range egg whites

½ tsp sea salt

Nicey Ricey Bars

A marshmallow rice crispie bar made with love and care is a remarkably easy, tasty treat to make. In these bars, the marshmallows are pre-toasted and slightly charred before being melted into the browned butter. If that's not enough, a layer of salted caramel drips through, creating a wonderland of sticky snap, crackle and pops.

Makes approximately 8–16 bars, depending on size

Butter and line a 20 cm (8 in) square, deep-sided baking tin. Leave 2.5 cm (1 in) flaps on all sides for easy removal.

Heat the grill (broiler) to its hottest setting and spread the marshmallows in a even layer on a large, rimmed baking sheet. Toast the marshmallows for about 1 minute or less. Keep a very close eye on them as they can catch extremely quickly. Set to one side to cool. For a charred taste, blowtorch patches of marshmallows until blackened.

In a large saucepan, make a brown butter (see page 54). Turn down the heat to low, tear off clumps of the toasted mallows and stir them into the browned butter. Cook until everything is melted and combined, stirring often.

Tip in the rice crispies and sea salt and stir well, coating every grain.

Spoon half of the mixture into the bottom of the prepared baking tray and press down. Drizzle the salted caramel over and top with the rest of the crispie mix.

Sprinkle over the 60 g (2 oz/⅔ cup) of marshmallows and spread to an even layer. Place under the grill, as before, to melt and brown the mallows, taking the blowtorch to them once again, if desired.

Leave to set before turning out and slicing. The bars will keep in an airtight container for up to 3 days, but are best eaten fresh!

200 g (7 oz/scant 1 cup) salted butter, plus extra for greasing

300 g (10½ oz/3½ cups) white mini marshmallows + 60 g (2 oz/⅔ cup) for topping

150 g (5 oz/5 cups) rice crispies (puffed rice)

1 tsp sea salt

150 g (5 oz) Classic Salted Caramel Sauce (see page 32)

Honey Nut Flapjacks

Makes 8 flapjacks

The day I moved into the railway arch in Deptford, London, with Richard, who runs the BluTop Ice Cream company, there was scant around for breakfast and after an early start I was hungry like the wolf. Enter a haphazard recipe of chewy honeyed flapjacks muddled with crunchy cornflakes, peanuts and salty caramel. Unashamedly, we ate huge hunks with Richard's cereal milk and marshmallow ice cream.

175 g (6 oz/¾ cup) salted butter, plus extra for greasing

100 g (3½ oz/generous ½ cup) soft light brown sugar

55 g (2 oz/scant ¼ cup) good-quality honey

½ tsp sea salt

100 g (3 ½ oz/1 cup) jumbo rolled oats

125 g (4 oz/1¼ cups) instant oats (oatmeal)

55 g (2 oz/scant 2 cups) cornflakes

50 g (2 oz/⅓ cup) peanuts, lightly crushed

100 g (3½ oz) Classic Salted Caramel Sauce (see page 32), warmed to a liquid

Preheat the oven to 160°C (325°F/Gas 3). Grease and line a 20 cm (8 in) square baking tin or silicone mould.

In a medium saucepan, melt the butter with the brown sugar, honey and sea salt, bring to a brief bubble, then remove from the heat. Add both types of oats and stir well, ensuring every oat is sticky and incorporated. Spoon two-thirds of the mix into the prepared tin, form an even layer and compress well with the back of a spoon.

Gently fold the cornflakes and crushed peanuts through the remaining one-third of flapjack mixture and spoon on top of the previous layer. Gently press down, being careful not to over compress.

Drizzle over the liquid salted caramel sauce and bake for 15 minutes or until light golden brown. These can catch easily so keep an eye on them towards the end of cooking.

Leave to cool in the pan. For a clean cut, chill in the fridge for 30 minutes before turning out and slicing.

Store in an airtight container at room temperature for up to 3 days.

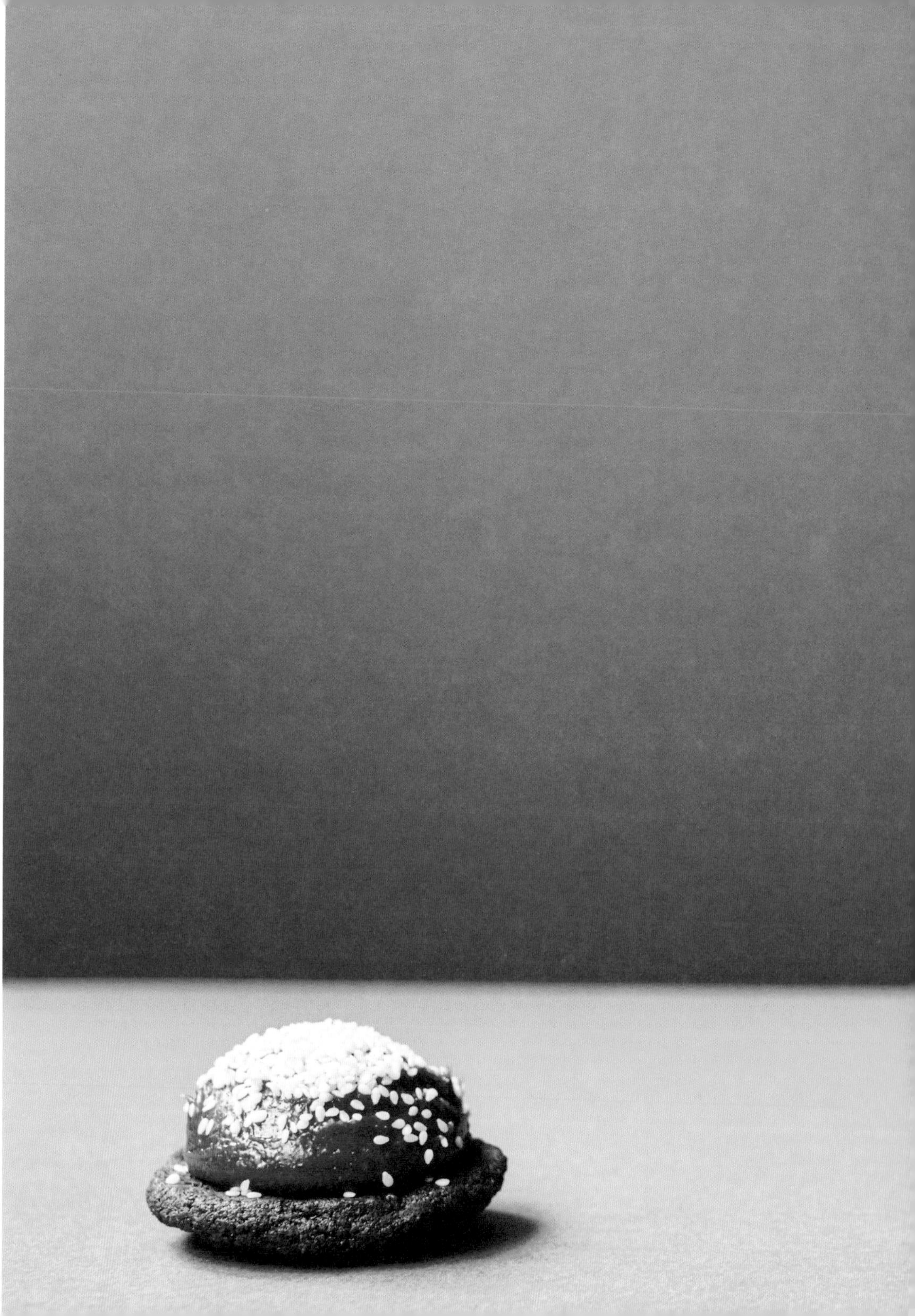

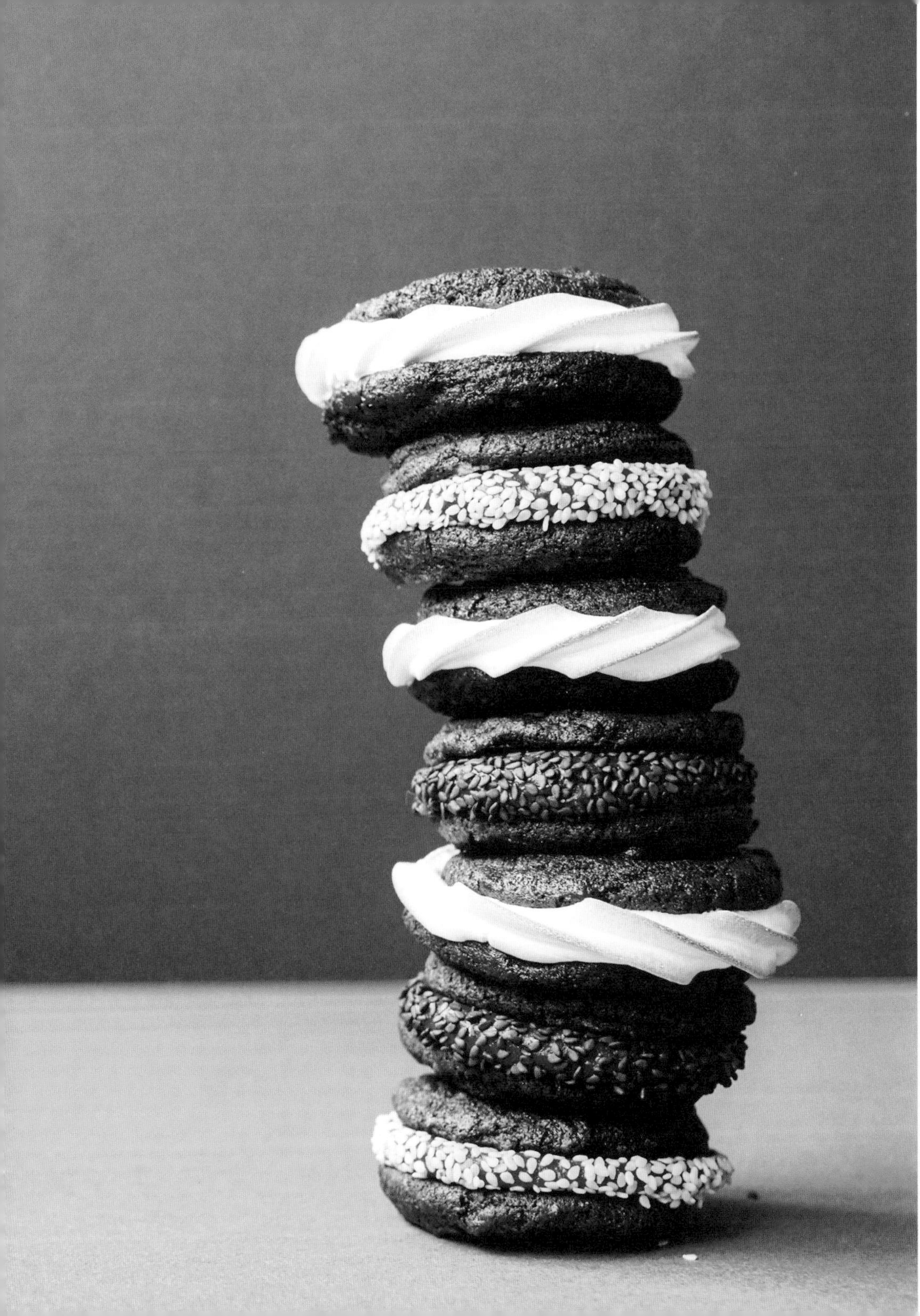

Dark Chocolate Cookies

These basic chocolate cookies are ideal for making sandwich cookies. I have included two options below, one for Tahini Cookies and the other for Goozeys (so named for being both gooey and oozey!). The Tahini Cookies, unless made in deep midwinter, are best kept in the fridge, or you risk a melty mess on your hands, whereas the Goozeys are best kept at room temperature to keep their caramel soft.
See photo on previous page.

Makes about 16 cookies

Preheat the oven to 150°C (300°F/Gas 2) and line 2 large baking sheets with baking parchment.

In a large bowl or a stand mixer, cream together the softened butter, both sugars and sea salt, scraping down the sides of the bowl as you go. Once pale and fluffy, beat in the egg.

Sift together the flour, cocoa powder and bicarbonate of soda. Add the dry ingredients to the creamed mix and beat on a low speed until just combined.

Add the chopped chocolate and beat on a medium speed to bring together to a soft dough.

Using a 1 tablespoon measure or number 50 portioner (see page 12), scoop out and place 2.5 cm (1 in) apart on the prepared baking sheets. Bake for 10 minutes, or until spread and slightly puffed.

Leave to cool on the baking sheets for 5 minutes. Lift the cookies, while still on the baking parchment, to 2 large cooling racks. Leave to cool completely on the paper, then transfer the paper and cookies to a flat surface and remove each cookie with a cookie lifter or steel spatula. This way the chocolate is set enough to lift cleanly.

125 g (4 oz/½ cup) salted butter, softened

175 g (6 oz/scant 1 cup) dark soft brown sugar

25 g (1 oz/2 tbsp) caster (superfine) sugar

½ tsp sea salt

1 large free-range egg

175 g (6 oz/1¼ cups) plain (all-purpose) flour

25 g (1 oz/scant ¼ cup) cocoa (unsweetened chocolate) powder

1 tsp bicarbonate of soda (baking soda)

175 g (6 oz/generous 1 cup) finely chopped dark chocolate

Goozey Cookies

1 quantity Marshmallow Fluff
(see page 52)

16 tsp Classic Salted Caramel
Sauce (see page 32),
at room temperature

Scoop the marshmallow into a piping bag fitted with a 1 cm (½ in) nozzle. Pipe a fat marshmallow border all around the circumference of a cookie. Fill the middle with 1 teaspoon of salted caramel sauce. Taking another cookie, gently top and press down to affix, creating a sandwich. Continue until all the cookies are used up.

Using a small blowtorch, toast the exposed marshmallow.

The cookies can be stored in an airtight container at room temperature for up to 3 days.

Tahini Cookies

black or white sesame seeds,
for dipping

16 tbsp Tahini Caramel
(see page 38), at room temperature

Pour the sesame seeds into a small, deep dish.

Taking one cookie, scoop out 1 tablespoon of the tahini caramel and place in the middle of the cookie, pressing down gently to affix. Invert the cookie into the sesame seeds and press the caramel into the seeds, coating the caramel.

Taking another cookie, gently press onto the caramel, creating a sandwich. Continue until all the cookies are used up.

The cookies can be stored in an airtight container in the fridge for up to 3 days.

Peanut Turtles

My friend Will is seriously fussy, so when these cookies became his Fatties first-choice pick, I couldn't have been happier. He's been such a massive help along the way that this recipe is dedicated to him. May he always have a cookie to hand. A dense and chewy cookie, crunchy with peanuts, smothered in salted caramel and drowning in chocolate, these are seriously indulgent. I love them cold from the fridge.

Makes 15–16 turtles

Preheat the oven to 150°C (300°F/Gas 2). Line 2 large baking sheets with baking parchment.

Sift together the flour, cocoa and bicarbonate of soda into a bowl and add the salt. Set aside.

In the bowl of a stand mixer, cream the butter and both sugars until pale and fluffy. Beat in the egg until well combined, scraping down the sides as you go.

Briefly beat in the dry ingredients, making sure you have a soft, smooth dough but being careful not to overwork.

Put the lightly crushed but not powdered peanuts in a bowl. Scoop out portions of the cookie with a number 30 portioner (see page 12) or into 2 tablespoon-sized balls and roll in the peanuts. Space out on the prepared baking sheets, leaving room for expansion.

Bake for 14 minutes or until the cookies are spread and slightly crackled. Leave to cool on the baking sheets.

To decorate the cookies, put the caramel in a disposable piping bag and snip a 5 mm (¼ in) hole in the bottom of the bag. Zigzag the caramel over each cookie.

Melt the chocolate in a small heatproof bowl set over a pan of gently simmering water, making sure the bottom of the bowl does not touch the water, or in a microwave in a suitable container, until just melted but not hot. Leave to cool slightly before putting into a disposable piping bag. Snip a 3 mm (⅛ in) hole in the bottom and zigzag the chocolate over the caramel. Leave to set.

Store in the fridge for up to 3 days in an airtight container, between sheets of baking parchment.

150 g (5 oz/1¼ cups) plain (all-purpose) flour

55 g (2 oz/scant ½ cup) cocoa (unsweetened chocolate) powder

1 tsp bicarbonate of soda (baking soda)

½ tsp sea salt

115 g (3¾ oz/scant ½ cup) salted butter, at room temperature

100 g (3½ oz/scant ½ cup) caster (superfine) sugar

100 g (3½ oz/generous ½ cup) soft light brown sugar

1 large free-range egg

125 g (4 oz/generous ¾ cup) roasted, salted peanuts, roughly crushed or chopped

250 g (9 oz) Classic Salted Caramel Sauce (see page 32), at room temperature

150 g (5 oz) good-quality dark or milk chocolate, depending on preference

Alfajores

When I first started my stall on Druid Street Market in south London, it was July and rather warm. These delicate sandwich biscuits were a perfect sweet pick-me-up for a hot day. I'd sugar them when I arrived in the morning, leaving gridded icing sugar stencils on the tarmac. Although not traditional, I like to add desiccated coconut to the dough instead of rolling the finished cookie in it. Alternatively, try two tablespoons of toasted cocoa nibs, crushed, instead.

Makes 25 Alfajores

Preheat the oven to 150°C (300°F/Gas 2) and line 2 large baking sheets with baking parchment.

Add all the ingredients (except the yolks, desiccated coconut and dulce de leche) to the bowl of a food processor fitted with the blade attachment. Pulse until the mixture resembles a fine granular crumb. Add the cold yolks and pulse again to form a dough. Add the desiccated coconut and briefly pulse again to combine.

Lightly dust a work surface with cassava flour and turn out the dough. Roll out to 5 mm (¼ in) thickness. Cut out 50 × 5 mm (¼ in) circles, bringing the dough back together and re-rolling as necessary. Carefully transfer the delicate circles to the prepared baking sheets, leaving 5 mm (¼ in) between biscuits to allow for very slight expansion.

Bake for 8–10 minutes or until the biscuits are dry but not coloured.

Leave to cool on the baking sheets. Sandwich pairs of cookies together with 1 teaspoon dulce de leche and dust with icing sugar.

Store in an airtight container at room temperature for up to 3 days.

115 g (3¾ oz/¾ cup) plain (all-purpose) flour

85 g (3 oz/⅔ cup) cassava flour, plus extra for rolling

seeds from 1 vanilla pod (bean)

60 g (2 oz/½ cup) icing (confectioners') sugar, plus extra for dusting

¼ tsp baking powder

115 g (3¾ oz/½ cup) salted butter, cold and cubed

2 large free-range egg yolks, fridge cold

30 g (1 oz/⅓ cup) desiccated (dried shredded) coconut

125 g (4 oz) Dulce de Leche (see page 36), at room temperature

Cowpat Cookies

Makes 16 cookies

So named for being the ugliest cookie around – so ugly but so darn delicious. These are a great way of using up Classic Chewy Salted Caramels offcuts (see page 28). Like a cookie florentine, these are crunchy and chewy and great with a cup of coffee after dinner.

115 g (3¾ oz/½ cup) salted butter

1 large free-range egg

70 g (2¼ oz/scant ⅓ cup) caster (superfine) sugar

70 g (2¼ oz/scant ⅓ cup) soft light brown sugar

1 tsp vanilla extract

90 g (3¼ oz/ scant ¾ cup) plain (all-purpose) flour

½ tsp sea salt

½ tsp bicarbonate of soda (baking soda)

45 g (1¾ oz) Classic Chewy Salted Caramels (see page 28), finely cubed

50-100 g (2-3½ oz) good-quality dark chocolate, chopped

In a small saucepan, melt the butter over a low heat, then remove it from the heat and leave to cool slightly.

In the bowl of a stand mixer fitted with the whisk attachment, or in a large bowl by hand, whisk together the egg, both sugars and the vanilla extract until the mixture falls in thick ribbons from the whisk, scraping down the sides of the bowl as necessary.

With the mixer running on medium, stream in the melted butter, then turn the mixer up to high for a short burst to quickly and fully incorporate the butter.

Using a wooden spoon or spatula, fold in the flour, salt, bicarbonate of soda, caramel pieces and chocolate.

Cover the bowl with cling film (plastic wrap) and chill in the fridge for 30 minutes, or until firm. Line 2 large baking sheets with baking parchment. Scoop out 1 tablespoon portions of the dough on to the prepared baking sheets, making sure there is plenty of room between cookies to allow for spreading.

Return to the fridge and chill for 2 hours or up to 2 days.

When ready to bake, preheat the oven to 160°C (325°F/Gas 3).

Bake the cookies for 10 minutes or until spread and the caramel has melted. Cool the cookies on the baking sheets.

These cookies are best eaten within 3 days of making and should be stored in an airtight container.

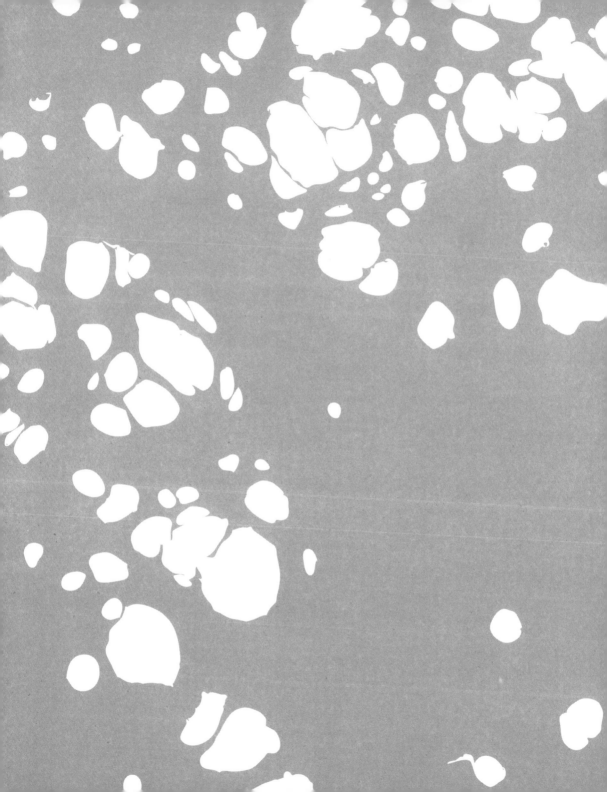

Total Indulgence

Time to pull on those stretchy party pants and really give in …

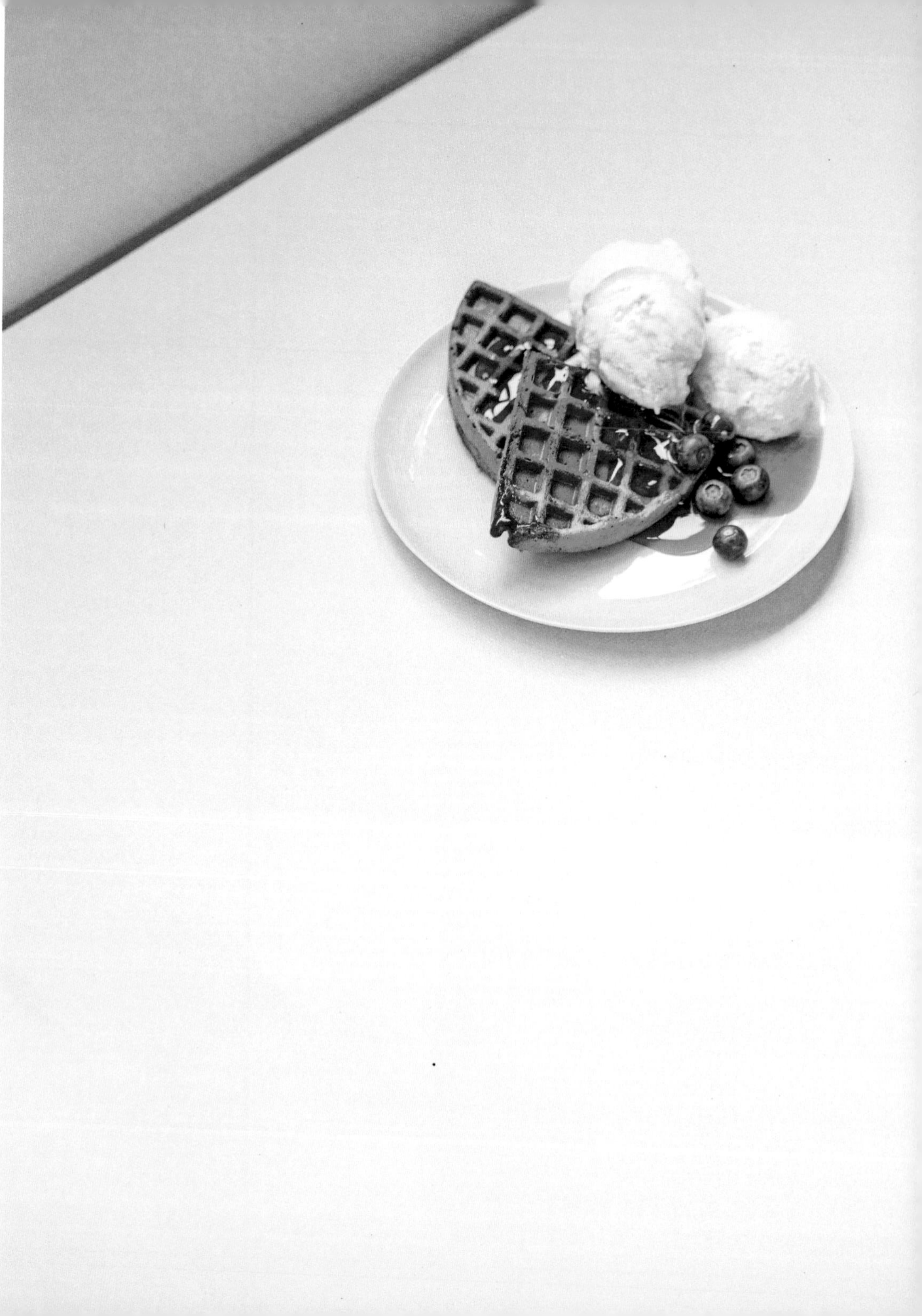

Total Indulgence ~ p.104

Caramelised Gingerbread Waffles

Makes 6–8 waffles,
depending on size and brand
of waffle maker

Throughout the process of writing this book I was told not to 'waffle on' or 'no waffling'. If you've ever been by the stall you'll know I'm an insatiable chatterbox, but I'll try to keep things succinct here. I LOVE WAFFLES. Especially these slightly tangy, crunchy, gooey, caramel-flecked gingerbread waffles. I have given a guide amount of buttermilk in this recipe as the thickness varies from brand to brand, so you might need to add more or less to achieve the desired consistency. These are perfect served hot and fresh with ice cream, fresh fruit and maple syrup.

75 g (2½ oz/⅓ cup) caster (superfine) sugar

85 g (3 oz/scant ⅔ cup) plain (all-purpose) flour

85 g (3 oz/⅔ cup) dark rye flour

¼ tsp sea salt

30 g (1 oz/scant ¼ cup) soft light brown sugar

1–2 tbsp ground ginger

20 turns black pepper (optional)

1 tsp baking powder

250 (8½ fl oz/1 cup) buttermilk, plus more if required

1 large free-range egg

2 tbsp sunflower oil

1 tbsp black treacle (molasses)

Line a baking sheet with baking parchment.

In a small, heavy-based saucepan, make a light dry caramel with the sugar (see page 16). Pour out onto the prepared sheet or a silicone sheet. Leave to set before smashing up to small shards. Set to one side.

Preheat a waffle iron to a medium-high heat.

In a medium bowl, whisk together both of the flours, the sea salt, sugar, ginger, black pepper, if using, and baking powder.

In a medium jug, whisk together 250 ml (8½ fl oz/1 cup) of the buttermilk, the egg, sunflower oil and black treacle, mixing well to incorporate the treacle. Whisk the wet mix into the dry ingredients. The mixture should be the consistency of cake batter, if very thick, add more buttermilk. Finally, stir through the caramel shards.

Depending on the size of your waffle maker, fill the waffle iron with 4–5 tablespoons of batter, or follow the manufacturer's instructions. Cook the waffles until puffed and golden and the caramel is dark and bubbling.

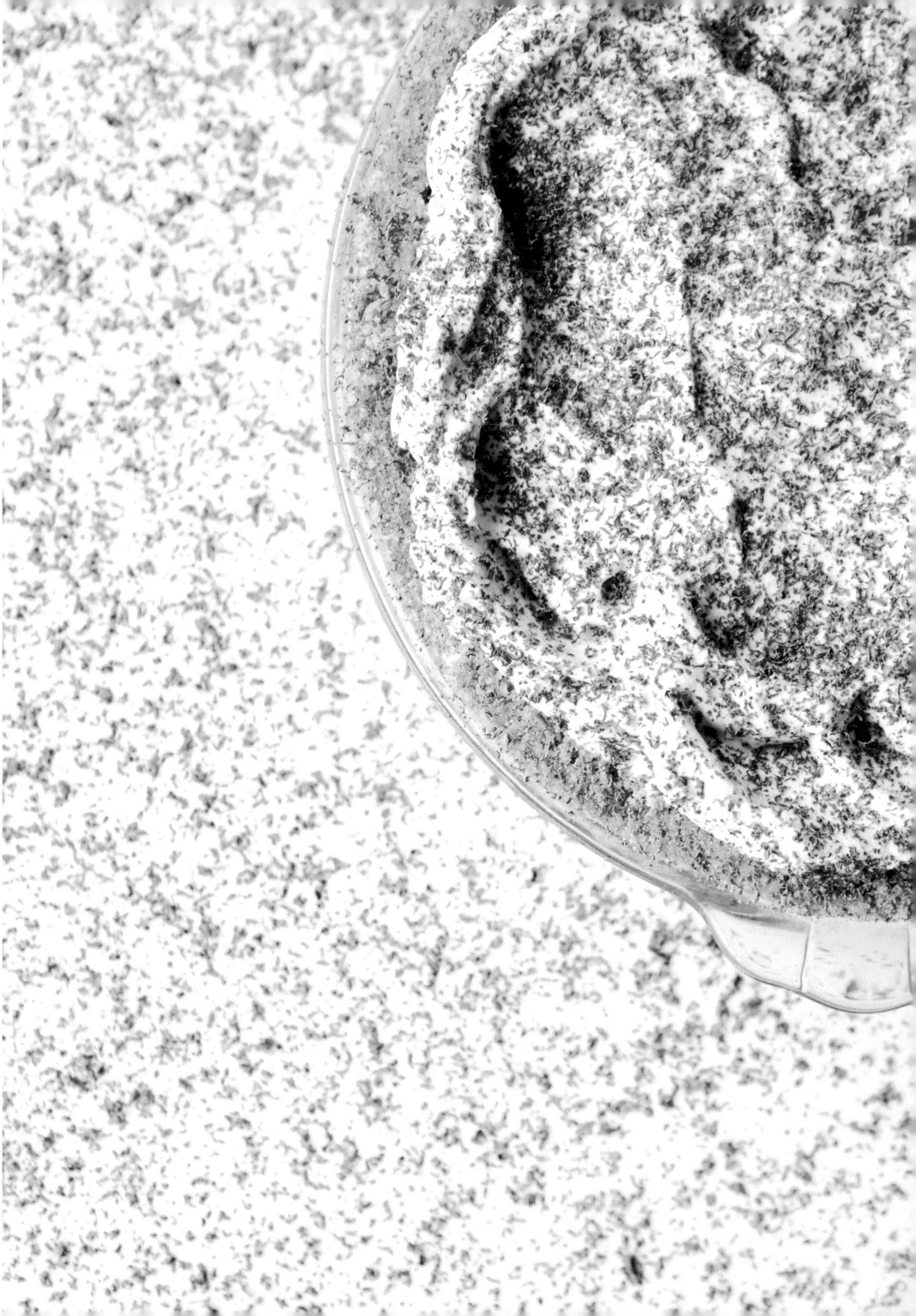

Total Indulgence ~ p.106

Banoffee Pie

This banoffee requires a little more work than the traditional 'a packet of this and a tin of that' pie, but I promise it's worth it. And for those that pass off banoffee as being tooth-achingly sweet, this one's for you. Salty pretzels in the crust, rich dark chocolate caramel and sour cream in the topping take this from 'just a tiny sliver' to 'seconds please!'

Start with the caramel layer. Make the chocolate salted caramel sauce following the instructions on page 32. Leave to cool in the pan while you make the pie crust.

To make the pie crust, melt the butter in a small saucepan, then set aside to cool slightly while you grind up the biscuits and pretzels in a food processor to a fine crumb. Add the melted butter and whizz again to dampen all the crumbs in the melted butter. Press the crumbs in an even layer into the bottom and up the sides of a loose-based 23 cm (9 in) flan ring, filling the scalloped edges evenly. Refrigerate for 20 minutes, or until firm.

After this time, the caramel should be cooled to room temperature and of a thick, pourable consistency. Remove the biscuit base from the fridge and pour and scoop the caramel into it, shaking and tapping to form an even layer. Return the flan ring to the fridge and chill for 20–30 minutes until the caramel is set.

Meanwhile, thinly slice the bananas and toss with the lime juice in a bowl. Cover with cling film (plastic wrap) and refrigerate.

For the cream topping, whip the ingredients until thick. Cover and refrigerate, if necessary, if still waiting for the caramel to set.

Once ready to assemble, arrange the bananas over the set caramel and top with the whipped cream, creating lovely swirls. If desired, grate over some chocolate and serve with bananas Foster caramel sauce. Serve right away or store in the fridge for a few hours before serving.

Caramel layer

500 g (1 lb 2 oz) Chocolate Salted Caramel Sauce (see page 32)

Pie crust

125 g (4 oz/generous ½ cup) salted butter

200 g (7 oz) digestive biscuits (graham crackers)

50 g (2 oz) salted pretzels

Banana layer

3 medium or 2 large bananas, you know how ripe you like them

juice of ¼ lime

Cream topping

200 ml (7 fl oz/generous ¾ cup) double (heavy) cream

100 ml (3½ fl oz/scant ½ cup) sour cream

½ tsp good vanilla paste or extract

Extras

good-quality dark chocolate, for grating (optional)

Bananas Foster Caramel Sauce (see page 43) (optional), at room temperature

Teurgoule

This is a very special rice pudding hailing from Normandy – it even has its own brotherhood that guards the official recipe. It is traditionally served with a Fallue, a type of brioche bread. The long, slow baking time gives this rice pudding its distinct, thick 'caramelised' crust (I think this might be our old friend Maillard at play again). Under the crust hides a golden custard layer and then the delicious sweet caramel rice. Very naughtily, I like mine with extra cream and dark plum jam (see recipe below).

Serves 8

Preheat the oven to 150°C (300°F/Gas 2).

Mix all of the ingredients except the nutmeg in a large, oven-safe, deep-sided dish. Grate the nutmeg over the top of the mixture.

Bake for 1 hour, then turn the oven down to 110°C (230°F/Gas ¼) and continue to cook for a further 5 hours, or until you have a thick, caramelised crust.

Leave for 30 minutes to settle, then serve warm.

1.5 litres (52 fl oz/6 cups) full-fat (whole) milk

500 ml (17 fl oz/2 cups) double (heavy) cream

150 g (5 oz/generous ⅔ cup) short-grain pudding rice

150 g (5 oz/⅔ cup) caster (superfine) sugar

½ tsp sea salt

seeds of 1 vanilla pod (bean)

1 cinnamon stick

¼ fresh nutmeg, grated

Dark Plum Jam

The sharpness and dark caramelisation of this quick compote perfectly offsets the richness of the rice pudding.

Makes about 150 g (5 oz)

Pit the plums, then roughly chop into small pieces, reserving as much juice as possible.

In a large, heavy-based saucepan, make a dark dry caramel with the sugar (see page 16). Carefully add the chopped plums and juice. Do not stir until the steam and sputtering has subsided.

Simmer over a low heat for about 10 minutes, stirring often until the mixture is thickened and is the consistency of a loose jam. It will thicken as it cools.

Leave to cool, then store in the fridge in an airtight container for up to 2 weeks.

6 small, ripe plums

100 g (3½ oz/scant ½ cup) caster (superfine) sugar

Miso Monkey Bread

Makes 1 large loaf

Fresh from the oven, this naughty bread is hard to resist, but resist you must. Wait and you will be rewarded with warm balls of sticky dough, salty with miso and crunchy with sesame seeds and walnuts.

Dough

85 g (3 oz/⅓ cup) salted butter

200 ml (7 fl oz/scant 1 cup) full-fat (whole) milk

550 g (1 lb 4 oz/generous 3⅔ cups) strong white bread flour, plus extra for dusting

2½ tsp fast-action dried yeast

50 g (2 oz/scant ¼ cup) caster (superfine) sugar

2 large free-range eggs

Miso butter

125 g (4 oz/½ cup) unsalted butter, plus 2 tbsp for greasing

50 g (2 oz) sweet white miso paste

225 g (8 oz/scant 1¼ cups) soft light brown sugar

2 tbsp black sesame seeds

50 g (2 oz/½ cup) walnuts

Start by making the dough. In a medium saucepan, melt the salted butter with the milk, then bring to a brief simmer. Set aside to cool slightly.

Meanwhile, in a bowl, whisk together the flour, yeast and sugar.

Whisk the eggs into the warm milk and butter, then add to the dry ingredients and pull together to form a dough. Leave to rest for 5 minutes.

Knead the mixture until a smooth and springy dough is formed. This will take about 5 minutes on a medium speed in a stand mixer fitted with a dough cook or 5–10 minutes by hand.

For the miso butter, melt the 2 tablespoons of unsalted butter in a small saucepan and thoroughly butter the inside of a large bowl and a 25 cm/2.8 litre (10 in/5½ pint) bundt tin using a pastry brush.

Place the dough in the buttered bowl, cover loosely with cling film (plastic wrap) and leave to rise in a warm place for 1 hour or until doubled in size.

Towards the end of the proving time, melt the remaining unsalted butter with the miso paste in a small pan. In a medium bowl, whisk together the brown sugar and sesame seeds.

In the bottom of your prepared bundt tin, pour in 2 tablespoons of the melted miso butter and sprinkle over 3 tablespoons of the sesame sugar. Top with the walnuts, spacing them out evenly.

Dip walnut-sized pieces of dough in the miso butter, then roll them in the sesame sugar. Place each into the tin, gently pressing into the dents of the bundt pan. Continue until the pan is evenly filled. If any sugar or butter remains, pour it over the top.

Cover the pan loosely with cling film and leave to rise again for 1 hour or until well risen.

Towards the end of the proving time, preheat the oven to 180°C (350°F/Gas 4) and line the middle shelf of the oven with foil to catch any drips. Bake for 30–35 minutes, or until well risen, golden and bubbling.

Allow to cool in the pan for 10 minutes before turning out onto a serving plate. Eat warm, tearing off ball by ball.

Bastardised Bee Sting Cake

This recipe is inspired by laziness and my most loyal customers, Carmen and Layth, who torture me with leaflets from La Glace in Copenhagen – a wonderful pastry shop – and stories of mountainous sweetened whipped cream. I wasn't getting a trip to Copenhagen any time soon, so I thought I'd better make my own lofty cream cake. I'd made a Bee Sting cake years ago and thought it a perfect place to start, although when I came to recipe testing I'd used all my honey reserves making the Honey Nut Flapjacks (see page 93). The nearest shop being a bus ride away, I reached for the best alternative, maple syrup, and the rest – as they say – is history. See photo on previous page.

Makes a 23 cm (9 in) cake

Begin by making the cake dough. In a large bowl, whisk together the flour, sugar, yeast and salt. Make a well in the middle and add the milk, eggs and melted butter. Stir with a wooden spoon or your hands until you have a loose, cohesive dough. Cover with cling film (plastic wrap) and leave to rise in a warm spot for 1 hour. The dough should be noticeably puffed.

During the last few minutes of the rise, butter a 23 cm (9 in) springform cake tin and line the bottom with baking parchment.

Once risen, transfer the dough to the prepared tin. With movement, the dough should deflate slightly. Gently tease the dough to cover the base of the tin. Cover again with cling film and leave to rise again for 30 minutes.

While the cake is rising for the second time, preheat the oven to 180°C (350°F/Gas 4) and make the almond topping. Place the butter, maple syrup, double cream and sea salt in a medium pan and melt together over a medium heat, stirring often. Bring the mixture to a simmer and continue to cook for about 5 minutes until the mixture turns light golden brown. Stir in the almonds and set to one side to cool slightly.

Once the cake has completed its second rise, evenly top the dough with the sticky almonds. This is made easier using 2 teaspoons to place little piles of sticky almonds all over the dough. The almond mixture may need to be warmed slightly if it is too stiff to handle.

Bake the cake for 20–25 minutes, or until golden and bubbling on top and a cocktail stick (toothpick) inserted in the middle comes out clean. Leave the cake in the pan and stand it on a cooling rack for 10 minutes before gently running a knife around the edge and removing the surround. Invert the cake and remove the baking parchment. Turn the right way up and leave to cool fully.

While the cake is cooling, make the caramel custard filling. Bring the milk up just to a simmer, remove from the heat but cover to keep warm. In a medium saucepan, make a dark dry caramel with the sugar (see page 16) and add the warmed milk, not stirring until the bubbling has subsided. Return to a low heat and stir until the caramel has dissolved. Whisk together the yolks, brown sugar and flour in a medium heatproof bowl. Return the caramel milk to the heat and bring up just to a boil before removing from the heat. Slowly pour over the yolk mixture, whisking all the time and mixing well to combine. Return the combined mixture to the pan and cook over a low heat, whisking all the time, until the consistency of a thick custard, bearing in mind that the custard will thicken further as it cools. Cover the surface of the custard with cling film and cool to room temperature before refrigerating to chill fully.

Once the cake is cooled and the custard is chilled, whip the cream and vanilla paste until thick, then spoon it into a large piping bag fitted with a wide nozzle of your choosing.

To assemble, slice the cake in half, placing the bottom layer on a cake stand or plate. Stir the custard to loosen slightly and, with a small offset spatula, smooth on top of the bottom cake layer into an even layer. Evenly pipe the cream to cover the custard, then top with the top almond cake half. Refrigerate the cake for 30 minutes–1 hour to firm up the cream slightly. Serve lightly chilled.

Leftovers can be stored in the fridge for 2–3 days, but this cake really is best eaten fresh, as with all good cream cakes.

Cake dough

300 g (10½ oz/2 cups) plain (all-purpose) flour

60 g (2 oz/¼ cup) caster (superfine) sugar

1½ tsp fast-action dried yeast

1 tsp sea salt, crushed to a fine grain

200 ml (7 fl oz/generous ¾ cup) full-fat (whole) milk, just warm to the touch

2 large free-range eggs

60 g (2 oz/generous ¼ cup) unsalted butter, melted, plus extra for greasing

Almond topping

100 g (3½ oz/generous ⅓ cup) salted butter

3 tbsp pure maple syrup

3 tbsp double (heavy) cream

1 tsp sea salt

150 g (5 oz/1½ cups) flaked (slivered) almonds

Caramel custard filling

300 ml (10 fl oz/1¼ cups) full-fat (whole) milk

125 g (4 oz/generous ½ cup) caster (superfine) sugar

4 large free-range egg yolks

30 g (1 oz/scant ¼ cup) dark soft brown sugar

40 g (1½ oz/⅓ cup) plain (all-purpose) flour

Cream layer

300 ml (10 fl oz/1¼ cups) double (heavy) cream

1 tsp vanilla paste or extract

Total Indulgence ~ p.114

Brown Butterscotch Cups

Serves 6 greedy people or
8 not so

I first discovered American-style pudding while
making Brooklyn Blackout Cake and am now hooked
on the stuff. I'm going to put it out there that I love
pudding skin and according to my Instagram quite
a few of you do, too – but if you don't, simply directly
cover the pudding with cling film (plastic wrap)
before chilling. This is a rich and creamy dessert; I like
to serve it with tangy crème fraîche, Goat's Curd
Butterscotch Sauce (see page 38), a sprinkle of
banana powder, a few crushed biscuits and extra sea
salt to offset the richness. Is it time for pudding yet?

60 g (2 oz/¼ cup) salted
butter

120 g (4 oz/⅔ cup) soft dark
brown sugar

60 g (2 oz/⅓ cup) soft light
brown sugar

250 ml (8½ fl oz/1 cup) full-
fat (whole) milk

550 ml (19 fl oz/2¼ cups)
double (heavy) cream

seeds from 1 vanilla pod
(bean)

1 tsp sea salt

20 g (¾ oz/scant ¼ cup)
cornflour (cornstarch)

5 large free-range egg yolks

In a large pan over a medium heat, brown the butter (see page 54). Add the sugars, swiftly followed by the milk and cream, then whisk to combine and to dissolve the sugars in the liquid. Add the vanilla seeds and sea salt and bring the liquid just to a simmer, whisking constantly to prevent scorching. Once simmering, remove from the heat and set to one side.

In a large bowl, whisk together the cornflour and egg yolks to form a paste. Slowly pour the hot base liquid onto the mixture, whisking well as you add.

Return the combined mixture to the pan and cook over a low-medium heat, whisking constantly and vigorously to avoid any lumps. Cook for about 4–6 minutes to the consistency of a thick custard.

Divide among chosen individual ramekins or glasses. Leave to cool to room temperature before chilling in the fridge until ready to serve. This will take at least 3 hours. The cups will keep for up to 3 days when kept in the fridge.

Chocolate Cake!

If ever there was a big cake to celebrate Fatties, this is it. It's packed full of my favourite things: dark chocolate, salted caramel and peanut butter.

I like to decorate the cake with reserved cake crumbs, toasted Marshmallow Fluff (see page 52) and clumps of shiny Cornflake Bocaditos (see page 58) but go wild with your own combinations of toppings. The frosting recipe makes a large amount, allowing you to go wild with piped decorations, too, if you so desire! See photo on page 139.

Makes a 23 cm (9 in) triple-layer cake

Preheat the oven to 170°C (340°F/Gas 3½).

Grease the sides and line the bottoms of 3 x 23 cm (9 in) round, springform cake tins.

First make the sponge. In a large jug, dissolve the espresso powder in the boiling water, then set aside to cool until just warm. Whisk in the melted butter and buttermilk.

In a large bowl, sift together the flour, cocoa, sugar, baking powder and bicarbonate of soda.

In the bowl of a stand mixer fitted with the beater attachment, beat the eggs on a medium speed until the whites and yolks are amalgamated. Turn the speed down to low and gradually pour in the liquids. Turn up the speed slightly and mix until well combined.

Returning to a low speed, add the flour mixture in thirds, scraping down the sides and bottom of the bowl as you go. Be careful not to overmix the batter, but beat until the batter is smooth and just combined.

Divide the batter among the prepared cake tins, gently tapping the cakes on a work surface to level the surface and get rid of any trapped air bubbles.

Bake for 35-40 minutes or until a thin skewer or cocktail stick (toothpick) inserted comes out streak-free but with a few moist crumbs attached. Ovens vary so it might be necessary to rotate the cakes during baking or adjust the baking time per cake.

Cool in the pans for 20-25 minutes, then remove from the pans, peel away the baking parchment and cool fully on cooling racks.

Make the frosting. Combine the softened butter, peanut butter, salted caramel, sea salt and vanilla extract in the bowl of a stand mixer fitted with the beater attachment. Beat on a medium speed until well blended and pale. Beat in the sugar in 4 stages, starting on a low speed, scraping down the bowl between additions. Increase the speed to high once all the sugar is added. Beat until pale and fluffy. If runny, add more sugar until the desired consistency has been achieved.

To assemble, place the cake layers on a flat, level cake board, surface or turntable and level the tops with a long, sharp serrated knife or cake leveller, cutting off the cracked dome. These can be reserved for crumbing and decorating the cake or are delicious cut into chunks and served with hot Salted Caramel Custard (see page 48) for a warming pudding.

Take one cake layer and top with 250–300 g (9–10½ oz) of the frosting, spread out to a flat, even layer.

Drizzle over the salted caramel sauce and dollop on some salted caramel peanut butter. Top with the next layer of cake and repeat the filling process as before, topping with the final cake layer, placed upside down for a smooth and flat finish.

Take a little of the frosting and with a small offset spatula, apply a thin layer of frosting all over the cake, using a cake scraper to smooth the surface. Scrape any excess frosting into a small separate bowl. Place the cake in the fridge or freezer for 15–20 minutes, or until no frosting comes away on your finger when gently touched.

With the remaining frosting, working as before apply a thicker layer of the frosting. Smooth first with the small offset spatula and then the cake scraper. Decorate as desired!

Sponge

2 tsp instant espresso powder

250 ml (8½ fl oz/1 cup) boiling water

175 g (6 oz/¾ cup) salted butter, melted

550 ml (19 fl oz/2¼ cups) buttermilk, at room temperature

425 g (15 oz/scant 3½ cups) plain (all-purpose) flour

265 g (9½ oz/generous 2½ cups) cocoa (unsweetened chocolate) powder

750 g (1 lb 10 oz/3⅓ cups) caster (superfine) sugar

2 tsp baking powder

4 tsp bicarbonate of soda (baking soda)

5 large free-range eggs

Frosting

450 g (1 lb) unsalted butter, softened, plus extra for greasing

500 g (1 lb 2 oz) smooth peanut butter

125 g (4 oz) Classic Salted Caramel Sauce (see page 32), at room temperature

1 tsp sea salt

2 tsp vanilla extract

650–750 g (1 lb 7 oz– 1 lb 10 oz/5¼–6 cups) icing (confectioners') sugar

Filling

(The amounts are up to you, depending on whether you want it demure or oozing)

Classic Salted Caramel Sauce (see page 32), at room temperature

Salted Caramel Peanut Butter (see page 62), at room temperature

Total Indulgence ~ p.117

Each Peach Pie

A juicy, cardamom-spiced pie, deep with caramel, tart with peaches and sweet with crunchy sugar and buttery pastry (see recipe photo on previous page). Demerara sugar works fine for this recipe, or you can use Turbinado, a large-grain, dry sugar with a light caramel flavour. This is perfect served with Salted Caramel Custard (see page 48) vanilla ice cream or Burnt Honey Whipped Cream (see opposite) – oh, and maybe a drizzle more caramel.

Makes a 23 cm (9 in) pie

Begin by making the pie crust. In the bowl of a food processor fitted with the blade attachment, pulse together the flour, sugar and butter until sandy. In short bursts, add the cold water, pulsing between additions. The pastry is ready when the crumbs pressed between finger and thumb form a dough.

Pour out the crumbs onto a large, clean work surface and bring together to form a dough. Divide the dough into 2 equal portions, press out to 15 cm (6 in) flat circular discs, wrap in cling film (plastic wrap) and refrigerate for 20 minutes, or until needed. The pastry can be stored for up to 2 days in the fridge. Just remove 10–20 minutes before rolling out.

Next, prepare the peach filling. Bring a large pan of water to the boil and fill a large bowl with iced water. Cut an cross-shape in the bottom of each peach. Blanch the peaches in pairs by lowering them into the boiling water for 20 seconds, using a large slotted spoon, then lifting them out and immersing them in the iced water. This should help loosen the peach skin to aid peeling. Peel the peaches and cut into quarters, discarding the pit.

In a large bowl, whisk together the plain flour, cornflour, caramel sugar, sea salt and ground cardamom. Toss the peaches in the dry ingredients, then set to one side.

Preheat the oven to 220°C (430°F/Gas 7). Line a large, flat baking sheet with foil and put it in the oven.

Roll out one of the pastry circles to fit a 23 cm (9 in) pie dish, then trim the edges, leaving a 2 cm (¾ in) overhang. Arrange the peaches to fit. Roll out the second disc, cut into lattice strips or cut

Pie double crust

400 g (14 oz/3¼ cups) plain (all-purpose) flour

15 g (½ oz/1 tbsp) caster (superfine) sugar

225 g (8 oz/1 cup) salted butter

100–125 ml (3½–4 fl oz/ scant ½–½ cup) cold water

Peach filling

6–7 nice peaches, half ripe

20 g (¾ oz/scant ¼ cup) plain (all-purpose) flour

20 g (¾ oz/scant ¼ cup) cornflour (cornstarch)

115 g (3¾ oz/½ cup) Caramel Sugar (see page 44)

¼ tsp sea salt

5–10 cardamom pods, deseeded and crushed

1 large free-range egg, beaten

Demerara or Turbinado sugar, for finishing

into a circle to fit, punching out a steam hole. Brush the overhanging pastry with the beaten egg, top with the top crust and pinch the bottom and top edges together to secure. Trim off any excess pastry to neaten the edges, if required. Re-roll any pastry scraps and cut out shapes to decorate, fixing them with the beaten egg. Brush with the remaining beaten egg and sprinkle over the sugar for a sweet and crunchy finish.

Place the pie on the preheated baking sheet and bake for 15 minutes, then turn the oven down to 190°C (375°F/Gas 5) and bake for a further 40 minutes or until the crust is a deep golden brown and the juices are thick and bubbling. Keep a close eye on the pie during baking. If the pastry starts to catch cover the pie with foil and continue to bake.

Remove the pie from the oven and leave to cool to room temperature.

Burnt Honey Whipped Cream

Makes 600 ml
(20 fl oz/2½ cups)

This is the type of recipe that, once stumbled upon, will have you making it just to eat a bowl; you will get two paces from the fridge and look back longingly, wondering if it is missing you as much as you are missing it, as lovers departing at a station. I prefer to whip this cream by hand – after all the hard work and time waiting, what a shame it would be to let a machine go mad and overbeat it. By hand, you have a better feel of when it's just perfect.

500 ml (17 fl oz/2 cups)
double (heavy) cream

100 g (3½ oz/scant ⅓ cup)
good-quality honey

1 tsp sea salt

Begin by gently warming the cream: it should be hot to the touch, but don't let it boil. Cover and keep warm.

Place the honey in a medium saucepan and set over a low-medium heat. Cook for 3–4 minutes until the honey darkens and begins to smell slightly burnt. Like making a dark caramel, hold your nerve here. Once darkened, add the salt and remove from the heat.

Add the warm cream to the honey, stirring well. Return to the heat and slowly bring the mix to a rolling simmer, stirring constantly to stop the bottom from catching. Bring to a brief boil, then remove from the heat immediately.

Pour the mix into a large bowl and cover with cling film (plastic wrap), pressing it onto the surface of the cream. Leave to cool to room temperature, then put in the fridge to cool completely (between 4–6 hours or until ready to whip).

When ready to serve, take the cream from the fridge and whip by hand until thick and luscious.

Caramelised Puff Tart

Makes a 20 × 30 cm
(8 × 12 in) tart

Deeply caramelised, crisp puff pastry and fluffy
clouds of whipped ricotta make a comely base for
an array of tempting toppings. I've included a few
ideas below, but go ahead and adorn it with whatever
floats your boat the highest.

Pastry

320 g (11 oz) ready rolled
puff pastry rectangle, or
equivalent

200 g (7 oz/scant 1 cup)
caster (superfine) sugar,
divided

Whipped ricotta

250 g (9 oz) ricotta

150 ml (5 fl oz/scant ⅔ cup)
double (heavy) cream

Remove the pastry from the fridge 10 minutes before you need to
use it to allow it to come just to room temperature.

Line a 20 × 30 cm (8 × 12 in) baking sheet with baking parchment,
folding around the edges to keep it down. Evenly sprinkle over
100 g (3½ oz/scant ½ cup) of the sugar.

Preheat the oven to 180°C (350°F/Gas 4).

Roll out or trim your pastry to 20 × 30 cm (8 × 12 in). Carefully
lay the pastry in the pan on top of the sugar, sprinkle over the
remaining sugar and cover with another piece of parchment and
another baking sheet. Chill in the fridge for 1 hour.

Leaving the baking sheets layered, bake in the oven for
30 minutes. After this time, the sugar should be starting to
caramelise around the edges. Remove the top pan and parchment
and bake for a further 15 minutes.

Leave to cool in the pan for 10 minutes, then very carefully turn
over and peel away the bottom parchment. A gloriously golden
crust should greet you. Leave to cool fully while you make the
ricotta cream.

For the cream, simply whip the ricotta with the cream until soft
peaks form – by hand is better to avoid overbeating. Spoon the
cream onto the cooled puff and spread almost to the edges with a
small offset spatula.

Ideas for toppings

Fresh summer berries and Caramel Sugar (see page 44) or icing
(confectioners') sugar.

Sliced banana, warm Miso Salted Caramel Sauce (see page 32)
and dark chocolate shavings.

Fresh sliced plums and Dark Plum Jam (see page 108).

Pitted black cherries soaked in kirsch and warm Chocolate Salted
Caramel Sauce (see page 32).

Caramel Spiced Citrus Fruits

I couldn't escape without one really fruity recipe, a plentiful dish of vibrant citrus fruits sweetened with a lightly spiced caramel syrup. A really refreshing, vitamin-giving tonic of a dessert, not necessarily a total indulgence but a good way of dealing with too many of them.

Serves 2–4

Begin by making the spiced caramel syrup. In a small, heavy-based saucepan, make a dark dry caramel with the sugar (see page 16). Just as the caramel is beginning to shimmer and smoke, turn off the heat and very carefully add the water – it will bubble and steam. Stir until all of the caramel is dissolved in the water. Add the spices and return to a low heat to simmer for 3 minutes. Remove and set aside to cool.

Once the syrup is at room temperature, top and tail the fruits and, with a sharp knife, take off the peel and pith. Segment the small citrus fruits and slice the grapefruit and blood orange. Arrange on a platter and sprinkle over the lime juice. Strain the syrup and pour over the fruits.

The dish can be chilled in the fridge before serving or served at room temperature. Decorate with freshly torn mint leaves.

4 tangerines, clementines or mandarins

1 white or ruby red grapefruit

1 large blood orange

juice of ½ lime

fresh mint leaves, to garnish

Spiced caramel syrup

100 g (3½ oz/scant ½ cup) caster (superfine) sugar

100 ml (3½ fl oz/scant ½ cup) just boiled water

1 small cinnamon stick

4 green cardamom pods, lightly bashed

2 black cardamom pods, lightly bashed

2 whole cloves

Pecan Pinwheel Ice Cream Sandwiches

Serves 2–4

These tempting little pinwheel-shaped palmiers make the most adorably tasty mini ice-cream sandwiches, especially when paired with BluTop Ice Cream's recipe for salty caramel, brown butter ice cream or 'Fat Man Scoop' as we like to call it (see page 126). Drizzle over extra Brown Butter (see page 54) for an extra buttery flavour-hit.

320 g (11¼ oz) packet ready-rolled all-butter puff pastry (or equivalent)

75 g (3½ oz/¾ cup) pecans, very finely chopped

80 g (3 oz/1⅓ cup) caster (superfine) sugar, divided into 30 g (1 oz/2 tbsp) and 50 g (2 oz/scant ¼ cup)

20 g (¾ oz/1½ tbsp) soft light brown sugar

1 tsp sea salt

Remove the pastry from the fridge 10 minutes before you want to use it to allow it to come just to room temperature. This will make the pastry easier to work with and less prone to tearing when rolling. Remove the pastry from the packaging and unroll.

In a small bowl, mix together the pecans, 30 g (1 oz/2 tbsp) of the sugar, the brown sugar and sea salt. Sprinkle the mixture over the pastry, spreading it out in an even layer to the edges with your fingers. Lightly roll over the filling with a rolling pin to lightly compress it into the pastry.

From the shortest end, roll up into a fat sausage, keeping the roll fairly tight. Roll the sausage in baking parchment, twisting the ends to seal. Chill in the refrigerator for 1–2 hours or in the freezer for 20 minutes until completely cold and firm to the touch, but not frozen solid if using the freezer.

Preheat the oven to 160°C (325°F/Gas 3). Line 2 large baking (cookie) sheets with baking parchment.

For mini pinwheels, cut disks 5 mm (¼ in) wide. For larger pinwheels, cut slices 1 cm (½ in) thick and use a rolling pin gently to roll out and flatten. Spread out on the prepared baking sheets and sprinkle over the remaining 50 g (3 oz/⅓ cup) of sugar.

Bake for 25–30 minutes or until caramelised and golden. Remove from the oven and leave to cool on the baking sheets.

They can be stored for up to a week in an airtight container but will lose their crunch over time.

Fat Man Scoop

Don't let the length of this recipe put you off, with an ice cream maker and a little patience you'll be churning and cheering in no time!

Makes about 1 litre
(34 fl oz/4⅓ cups)

First, prepare a brown butter according to the instructions on page 54. Once foaming and golden, add the brown sugar and stir together so the butter is fully absorbed by the sugar. Leave to one side to cool. Once it reaches room temperature, cover the pan with cling film (plastic wrap) and place in the fridge to fully chill.

Next, make the salted caramel sauce for the ripple. In a medium saucepan make a dark dry caramel following the instructions on page 16. Remove the pan from the heat and add the cream and wait for the bubbling and spluttering to subside before stirring. If any undissolved lumps of caramel remain, return to a low heat and stir until all the caramel is melted. Add the sea salt. Put the pan of caramel into an ice bath or a sink of cold water and allow it to cool for around 10 minutes. Once cool, store at room temperature until needed.

For the ice-cream base, add the milk, cream and half of the sugar to a large pan over a low heat. Warm the mixture until the temperature reaches 40°C (104°F). Whilst the milk and cream mixture is warming, whisk together the skimmed milk powder and cornflour in a medium bowl. When the milk/cream mix reaches temperature, remove the pan from the heat and add around half of the mix to the skimmed milk powder and cornflour. Blend vigorously using an electric or hand-held whisk. Once smooth, pour through a fine sieve back into the pan of milk mix. Stir in the vanilla extract. Return the pan to a low heat and stir continuously with a heatproof spatula, scraping the bottom of pan to make sure the mixture doesn't catch. Heat gradually to 70°C (158°F), then remove from the heat.

Whisk the egg yolks and remaining sugar together in a medium bowl until slightly foamy. Temper the egg yolks by pouring a slow, thin drizzle of the hot milk mix over the egg/sugar mix while whisking constantly. This stops the eggs from cooking too quickly but brings them up to the same temperature as the mix. Once around half of the milk mix has been added to the egg yolk mix,

Brown butter

50 g (2 oz/scant ¼ cup) unsalted butter

50 g (2 oz/scant ⅓ cup) dark soft brown sugar

Salted caramel sauce

150 g (5 oz/heaped ¾ cup) caster (superfine) sugar

150 ml (5 fl oz/scant ⅔ cup) double (heavy) cream, warmed slightly

½ tsp sea salt

Ice cream base

540 ml (19 fl oz/2¼ cups) full-fat (whole) milk

210 ml (2½ fl oz/scant 1 cup) double (heavy) cream

130 g (4 oz/½ cup) granulated sugar, divided in half

55 g (2 oz/scant ½ cup) skimmed milk powder

25 g (1 oz/scant ¼ cup) cornflour (cornstarch)

2 tsp good-quality vanilla extract or paste

3 large free-range egg yolks

pour everything back into the pan through a sieve with the rest of the base, while stirring with the spatula.

Return the pan to a low heat once again and stir continuously, scraping the bottom of the pan, until the base thickens and reaches 85°C (185°F) – you're looking for the texture of a fresh custard. If the base is still too thin, just keep it on the heat for another minute and it will thicken very rapidly.

Once the base is thick, immediately plunge the pan into an ice bath. Leave the base to cool, stirring occasionally, until a thermometer reads 5°C (40°F). Cover with cling film (plastic wrap) and chill in the fridge for at least 4 hours or preferably overnight.

Once the base has aged, remove it from the fridge along with the brown butter. The brown butter mix should now have chilled fully and will have formed a sort of 'sugar patty'. Break the patty up into small pieces. Blend the base with a stick blender until smooth, then add the chunks of sugar patty. Blend again breifly, until the larger chunks of patty have been broken up into small, crunchy flecks.

Churn the brown butter-flecked base in an ice-cream machine according to the manufacturer's instructions (I recommend not filling the bowl of your ice cream machine over three-quarters of the way full).

Once the base is frozen, remove a couple of tablespoons of ice cream and place them in a plastic tub. Pour over a ripple of salted caramel then top with some more tablespoons of ice cream. Continue layering the ice cream and salted caramel until you've used all the ice cream. Place a lid on the tub and put it in the freezer to hard-freeze for at least 3 hours.

The ice cream is now ready to serve or can be stored in the freezer for up to 3 weeks.

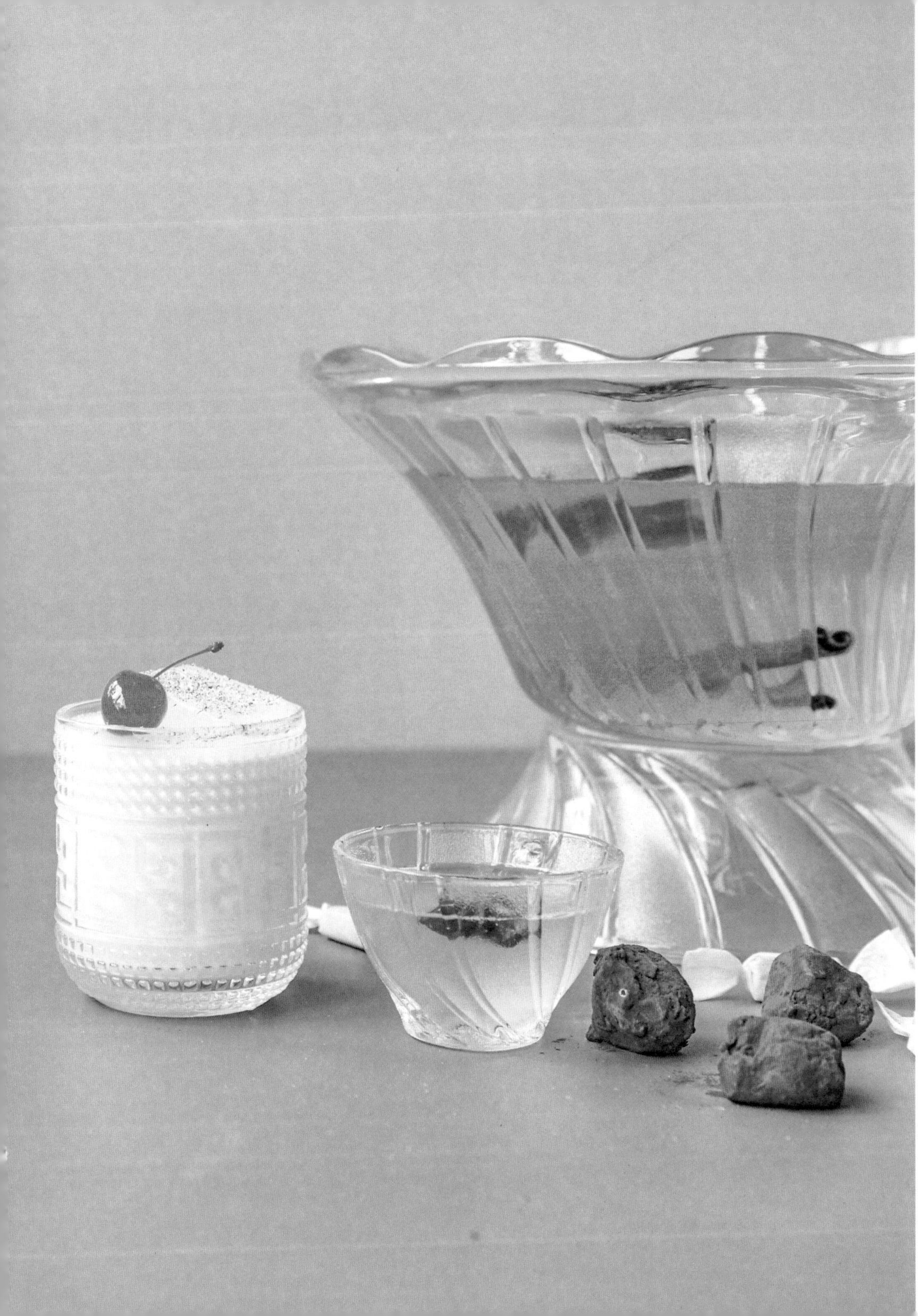

Total Indulgence ~ p.129

Flapjack Vodka

Not strictly salted caramel, but all the joys are there! Great served neat or in Flapjack Punch (see below).

Makes 750 ml (25 fl oz/3 cups)

Preheat the oven to 180°C (350°F/Gas 4).

Line a deep-sided baking dish with foil and pour in the oats, shaking to form an even layer. Toast in the oven for around 15 minutes, or until lightly golden and fragrant. Once toasted, remove from the oven and leave to cool until just warm to the touch.

Take a 1 litre (34 fl oz) clean Kilner (Mason) jar and add the vodka, sugar and salt. Shake well to combine. Add the warm oats and shake well again. Store in a cool, dark place for up to 5 days, shaking the jar twice a day to help the infusion. On the third day of storage, give the liquid a try. A subtle oat flavour will have developed. If you like it, strain, or for a stronger flavour leave for a couple more days.

To strain the mixture, line a fine mesh sieve with muslin (cheese-cloth) and place over a large, clean container. Once the liquid is passed, tip the oats into the muslin-lined sieve and, gathering up the sides of the fabric, twist to really wring out the oats – so much flavour lies in there!

Store the vodka in a clean, airtight bottle ready for pouring.

100 g (3½ oz/1 cup) old-fashioned rolled oats

750 ml (25 fl oz/3 cups) vodka

50 g (2 oz/⅓ cup) dark brown muscovado sugar

tiny pinch of sea salt (a little goes a long way here)

Tip

For a tasty decoration or breakfast topping, the sweetened vodka oats can be dried by baking in a low oven, about 100°C (230°F/ Gas ¼) for 10–15 minutes, or until just toasty. Leave to cool and store in an airtight container.

Flapjack Punch

This recipe is dedicated to Granny who, lacking a cocktail shaker, used an empty milk carton to shake Pisco Sours.

Serves 1

Measure all the ingredients (except the oats, if using, and nutmeg) into a cocktail shaker. Top up the shaker with ice. Shake well for 30 seconds or until the shaker is frosted.

Fill a tumbler with ice. Strain the punch over the ice into the glass and serve immediately. For added crunch and sweetness, top with a sprinkle of toasted oats or cinnamon, if using.

60 ml (2 fl oz/2¼ cups) Flapjack Vodka (see above)

2 tbsp double (heavy) cream

2 tbsp full-fat (whole) milk

2 tbsp Simple Caramel Syrup (see page 50)

ice cubes

grating of nutmeg (optional)

toasted oats from Flapjack Vodka (optional) (see above)

Spiced Caramel Apple Bourbon

Makes about 700 ml (24 fl oz/
generous 2¾ cups)

This makes a great tipple and adds a kick to the recipe for Mulled Caramel Apple Cider (see below).

50 g (2 oz/scant ¼ cup) caster
(superfine) sugar

1 small cinnamon stick

750 ml (25 fl oz/3 cups)
bourbon whisky

2 small red apples, unwaxed
or well washed

In a small, heavy-based saucepan, make a dark dry caramel with the sugar (see page 16). Pour out onto baking parchment. Leave to set before smashing up to small shards.

Take a 1 litre (34 fl oz) clean Kilner (Mason) jar and add the caramel shards, cinnamon stick and bourbon. Shake well to mix.

Core the apples and cut into eighths, but do not peel. Add the apples to the jar and give another good shake. Store in a cool, dark place for up to 1 month, shaking the jar twice a day to help the infusion.

To strain the mixture, line a fine mesh sieve with muslin (cheesecloth) and place over a large, clean container. Store the Bourbon in a clean airtight bottle ready for pouring.

Mulled Caramel Apple Cider

Serves 10 generously

Whenever I make this recipe I think of Rosie Burdock, from the novel Cider with Rosie, seducing Laurie Lee under a hay wagon after drinking from a flagon of cider. The recipe works best in an enamelled cast iron casserole pot with a lid (it stays warmer for longer).

200 g (7 oz/scant 1 cup)
caster (superfine) sugar

250 ml (8½ fl oz/1 cup)
good-quality apple juice

1 large cinnamon stick

½ nutmeg, freshly grated

1 vanilla pod (bean), scraped
seeds and pod

2 star anise

4 cloves

2 litres (70 fl oz/8 cups)
scrumpy cider

200 ml (7 fl oz/scant
1 cup) Spiced Caramel Apple
Bourbon (see above) or
Calvados (optional)

In a large heavy-based pan, make a medium-dark dry caramel with the sugar (see page 16). Deglaze the caramel with the apple juice, watching out for splutters. Stir until the caramel is dissolved, then add the spices.

Bring the mix to a gentle simmer for 8–10 minutes until you have a thick syrup. Turn off the heat and add 500 ml (17 fl oz/2 cups) of the cider, then add the remaining cider and bring up to a gentle simmer for a few minutes, stirring to dissolve the syrup. Do not boil! Remove from the heat, cover the pot and leave to infuse for a few hours. To serve, gently warm the liqid without boiling and serve in punch cups.

Once you are ready to serve, warm up the cider and add the bourbon or Calvados, if using. Ladle into heatproof glasses and serve warm.

Store the bourbon in a clean airtight bottle ready for pouring.

Coffee + Doughnut
Milkshake

Salted Caramel
Peanut Butter Milkshake

Chocolate Malt
Milkshake

Bananas Foster
Milkshake

Milkshakes

Choose a good-quality ice cream, a tub that feels heavy in your hand. Remove the ice cream from the freezer a few minutes before it's needed to allow it to become the texture of soft serve, but do not let it melt. See photos on previous page.

All recipes serve 1–2

Coffee + Doughnut Milkshake

Serve with a mini doughnut and drizzle over Classic Salted Caramel Sauce (see page 32), warmed to a pouring consistency.

500 ml (17 fl oz/generous 2 cups) vanilla ice cream

50 ml (2 fl oz/3 tbsp) cold brew coffee concentrate, or cooled espresso

1–2 tbsp fresh coffee grounds

3 tbsp coffee liqueur (optional)

Combine all the ingredients in the jug of a blender. Blend until smooth. Serve.

Salted Caramel Peanut Butter Milkshake

Top with extra crushed peanuts and whipped cream.

500 ml (17 fl oz/2 cups) vanilla ice cream

50 ml (2 fl oz/3 tbsp) full-fat (whole) milk

2 heaped tbsp Salted Caramel Peanut Butter (see page 64)

1–2 tbsp roasted salted peanuts

2 tbsp nut liqueur (optional)

Combine all the ingredients in the jug of a blender. Blend until smooth. Serve.

Chocolate Malt Milkshake

Bananas Foster Milkshake

I like to disguise this as Guinness and top with double cream. Very naughty!

I'm just bananas for the rum in this recipe, but if you're not, feel free to go virgin.

500 ml (17 fl oz/2 cups) dark chocolate ice cream

75 ml (2½ fl oz/⅓ cup) milk stout, ice cold

1 tbsp malted milk powder

250 ml (8½ fl oz/1 cup) vanilla ice cream or frozen yoghurt

50 ml (2 fl oz/3 tbsp) full-fat (whole) milk

2 bananas, peeled and frozen

2 tbsp Bananas Foster Caramel Sauce (see page 43), at room temperature

¼ tsp ground cinnamon

2 tbsp dark rum (optional)

whipped cream, for topping (optional)

Combine all the ingredients in the jug of a blender. Blend until smooth. Serve.

Combine all the ingredients in the jug of a blender. Blend until smooth. Serve.

About Chloe Timms

Self-confessed caramel snob Chloe Timms was born in Yorkshire, survived boarding school and gained a first class degree in 70s crafts before turning her hand to all things sticky and delicious. Chloe founded Fatties Bakery, a small London bakery dedicated to salted caramel confectionery and baked goods in 2015, following a period of 'what am I doing with my life!?' She found solace and solution in sugar and on a wing and a prayer she quit her job in fashion and turned full-time to creating the best treats she would like to eat. Luckily others enjoyed them too and she hasn't looked back since. She trades regularly at markets and events in London, and dreams of a bricks and mortar store.

Thank You

Daddy, thank you for inspiring me along this path. I miss you everyday. Mum, thank you for looking after me and giving me the space and freedom to grow Fatties and write this book. It means more than you can know.

To the book team: Kajal, River and all the team at Hardie Grant, thank you for making my dream a reality; Justin, you were the only designer I trusted with this project and I'm so glad to have had you by my side. You went above and beyond to make this book something we will both treasure; to the awesome ladies at Ginger Whisk for the incredible props!

Rebecca, thank you for putting up with my shouting and rude finger. Your patience is admirable as is your friendship. Thank you also for the killer recipe.

Will, thank you for all your guidance and creativity. It's lovely to have someone to get super excited over an idea with.

Elle, my safest pair of hands! Thank you for all your hard work and support, you're a treasure possum, you Flaming Galah!

Dicky, it's been a tricky time since I moved into the arch, you've been wonderfully ridiculous and made me laugh so much when I could have cried.

Cat, you've got my back and it means the world to me!

Carmen and Layth, you guys are awesome. It makes my day when I see your faces popping through the market. You're the funniest and most understanding customers a gal could ask for, and the sweetest couple.

To all the friends I have made since I followed the sticky path, and to all of those friends that have invested their time in this book with only cookies and crumbs for payment, thank you!

To all the strong women who inspired, and continue to inspire me to strike out on my own, thank you; you know who you are.

About Chloe Timms + Thank You ~ p.139

Index

Salted Caramel Dreams
by Chloe Timms

First published in 2017 by Hardie Grant Books

Hardie Grant Books (UK)
52-54 Southwark Street
London SE1 1UN

hardiegrant.com

Hardie Grant Books (Australia)
Ground Floor, Building 1
658 Church Street
Melbourne, VIC 3121

hardiegrant.com

British Library Cataloguing-in-Publication Data. A catalogue record for this book is available from the British Library.

ISBN: 978-1-78488-1-122

Publisher :
Kate Pollard

Commissioning Editor :
Kajal Mistry

Editorial Assistant :
Hannah Roberts

Publishing Assistant :
Eila Purvis

Photographer :
River Thompson

Art Direction :
Justin Hallström

Retouching :
Butterfly Creatives LTD and
River Thompson

Copy editor :
Wendy Hobson

Proofreader :
Kay Halsey

Indexer :
Cathy Heath

Colour Reproduction by p2d

Printed and bound in
China by 1010

10 9 8 7 6 5 4 3 2 1